COMMUNITIES OF THE ALONE

Communities

WORKING WITH SINGLE ROOM

of the Alone

OCCUPANTS IN THE CITY

By Joan Hatch Shapiro

ASSOCIATION PRESS

NEW YORK

COMMUNITIES OF THE ALONE

Standard Book Number: 8096-1810-9

Library of Congress Catalog Card Number: 79-129438

Printed in the United States of America

for Danny

Life is always surprising us, not by its
rich seething layer of bestial refuse—
but by the bright, healthy, and creative
human powers of goodness that are forever
forcing their way up through it. It is
those powers that awaken our indestructible
hope that a brighter, better and more humane
life will once again be reborn.

—MAXIM GORKY
My Childhood

Contents

Contents

Preface

This book is addressed to all those who have the potential power to influence the lives of single, sick people living in squalor and despair in our midst: their middle-class neighbors, whose attitudes ultimately sanction or forbid changes in housing, welfare and health patterns of care affecting the single room occupants; city planners and architects whose vision of future central cities must include housing for this overlooked population, for only at the peril of the central cities are they ignored; the creators of future welfare legislation, the current form of which directly enhances the pathology it was designed to ameliorate; welfare workers, on whom falls the final social responsibility for the SRO dwellers, and who can, under certain circumstances, admirably carry their responsibility forward; hospital administrators and medical staffs who must find the money, time, and patience to extend care to those who cannot come to search it out; the behavioral scientists who have, in the single room occupants, new territory to be explored, and to whom this book may offer a primitive map; and finally, social workers, whose profession will be largely shaped by its capacity to shift its priorities to "where the action is," in finding and helping unserved and suffering populations and stimulating social action to change their social and legal rights.

The least adequate members of the human group will continue to gather in our central cities, homeless and in need. They can neither be legislated, institutionalized, organized, nor wished out of existence. The well-intentioned hope of the service professions to resocialize SRO dwellers into the mainstream of American culture has ricocheted and will continue to do so. The social work profession can, however, enlarge the SRO dwellers' choices, strengthen their ties to services and to their neighborhood, support those few who are able to move into the working class, and institutionalize those who endanger the community itself. It remains the task of others among the poor and among the helping professions to change the social causes to which this crippled population constitutes an end point.

Our job is to preserve the strengths and the moments of beauty in the lives of these castoffs, to ease their pain and preserve them from being preyed upon, both by members of the underworld in their midst and by the larger world which seeks to sweep them out of sight in a mindless pattern of eviction and relocation.

Human beings are so constituted that invisible pain does not move us to action. But the SRO dwellers, in their pain, despair, and ugly eruptions of violence, have produced enough discomfort, anger, and fear in others to make themselves noticed. We have tried to respond. This book is the story of these efforts.

J. H. S.

Acknowledgments

Many concepts in this book derive from others; their ideas, attitudes or actions have become integral to my perception of the single room occupancy world and to participation in it. Their words and ways are buried in the work beyond attribution. They shared in the excitement of discovery, and gave generously from their own rich observations.

Nathan Lefkowitz, sociologist on the research staff of the Division of Community Psychiatry of St. Luke's Hospital Center from 1964 to 1968, first recognized and helped me to believe that we had stumbled upon an intervention model the astonishing impact of which could only be explained by its congruence with the life-style in the SROs.

Professor William Schwartz of the Columbia School of Social Work, whom we came to know after the method of intervention had been developed, legitimated our work within the fields of social work. He also showed me the beauty and drama of the workers' process records as a projective screen and taught and influenced deeply most of the student-workers in the project.

Of the hundreds of SRO tenants I came to know, three have had a very special role. John Farrow, Mary Pierce and Mickey Senior befriended me in my own project building and, with the utmost patience and wisdom, taught me how to become helpful.

My fellow workers, largely social work students, struggled to acculturate themselves in the SROs in order to give help—an agonizing process which they shared with me; they permitted me to perceive the steps of their learning and enabled me to reflect critically about my own experience as an SRO worker. Their records, used in altered form to preserve anonymity, create the

vivid clothing for the book. The workers are Josh Fendel, Kathy
Finn, Deborah Glassman, Billie Gleissner, Grace Jessen, Mary
Pierce, Chuck Sanders, Enid Schreibman and Sam Siris.

The members of a West Side Committee for Alcoholism,
which was formed before the first SRO project in 1962, have
continued through the years to be close colleagues and friendly
critics. They are Edna Baer and Carroll Novick of the Neighborhood Conservation Bureau, Ruth Schwartz of the Community
Service Society, and finally, and most especially, Lillian Zerwick
of the Amsterdam Welfare Center, whose vision of what welfare
service for SRO tenants could be I hope I have succeeded in
reflecting.

Dr. John Cotton, Director of the Department of Psychiatry,
Dr. Alan Elkins, Director of its Division of Community Psychiatry, and Mr. Charles Davidson, the Director of the St. Luke's
Hospital Center, have supported the work over the last five
years. They continually made exceptions and created new procedures to fit our needs in carrying out this unorthodox and unpredictable kind of work. Miss Esther Watson unscrambled, de-
coded and retyped various drafts with pleasure and good humor.
The final manuscript was expertly prepared by Mrs. Muriel
Golden.

Those who have read, edited and criticized part or the whole
of various drafts are: Professor Bernard Barber of the Sociology
Department of Barnard College, Janet Stokes and Barbara Hoff-
berg of the Research Staff of the St. Luke's Hospital Center, and
my close friend, Jean Mostkoff.

Above all, my husband, Dr. Daniel Shapiro, supported me
throughout the writing and lent his faith and persistence to help
me see the job to its ending. He has been its chief editor. My
children have patiently waited and given up our time together
until the book was finished.

Introduction

Urban industrial society rewards its contributors and institutionalizes its sick, disruptive and bizarre members. But caught between the fit and grossly unfit, a large population spins out its existence in limbo. It is made up of single, unattached poor people characterized by marked social and psychological maladaptation and chronic physical disease; often they are neither sick nor deviant enough to be institutionalized nor well enough to use health, social and welfare services effectively. Many cluster in the urban rooming houses or hotels known in New York City as Single Room Occupancy buildings, or SROs, where untreated illness, hunger, loneliness and sporadic violence are unrelieved regularities of existence.

The term SRO (Single Room Occupancy) refers to tenement apartment buildings which have been converted into living quarters for unattached poor people. They are, in effect, the slum hotels providing transient and permanent homes for alcoholics, addicts, prostitutes, petty criminals, the indigent chronically ill, the mentally retarded adult, the mentally ill, and the elderly—all people who cannot adequately care for themselves in the larger society. The SRO is New York City's way of housing these urban rejects. There are over 400 such buildings, housing about 30,000 people, the majority of whom are welfare recipients. Other cities—Chicago, Seattle, Boston, Paterson and Washington—have similar patterns of clustered housing for their marginal, unattached poor populations, but these are not separated from the Skid Row area as they are in New York.

While two-thirds of the city's SROs are well-managed and provide adequate housing for a single population and are socially accepted in their immediate neighborhoods, there are others with marked physical deterioration and conspicuous antisocial behavior.

Considerable community attention has been focused on these buildings. They cause what is known as the "SRO problem." It is a serious one for their neighborhoods, for the health and welfare agencies, and for the individuals residing in such buildings.

For the neighborhood, these SROs represent pockets of blight. They are sources of disturbances, crime and spreading deterioration on the blocks where they are located. The front stoops are natural places of congregation where drunks and addicts are frequently observed; boisterousness and street fighting are not uncommon. Other residents on the block are concerned for their safety. Communities in the process of neighborhood improvement are faced with the dilemma of how to deal with this problem. Removal of such SROs only disperses the population to other areas; yet continuance of them under the present circumstances vitiates any serious steps toward community improvement and stability.

Sporadically, such buildings have aroused neighborhoods sufficiently so that political action is taken to shut them down. When successful, the population then is scattered to other SROs and an endless, costly, and heartbreaking pattern emerges in which each neighborhood tries to sweep away its undesirables. This pattern continues in 1971 in those buildings where no intervention has been attempted.

The SRO tenant typically is untreated or undertreated. The SRO tenant is seldom the long-term client or patient of a helping professional. Profoundly alienated, clinically depressed, poorly nourished, chronically ill, economically dependent, typically he behaves in a manner which does not elicit helping responses. If he arrives at the beginning of a help-seeking track at all, he is painfully shy, is unable to state his problem clearly, and has little tolerance for waiting. He is a poor informant, misunderstands procedures, and follows recommendations or directions haphazardly. Therefore, he is labeled "unmotivated."

Among the poor he is given the lowest priority for receiving help: children, families, the aged and those with special disabilities elicit more public sympathy.

Nevertheless, he is an expensive citizen. He is the state hospital patient between hospitalizations, each successive hospitalization involving dozens of professionals. He is the addict between arrests or detoxifications. He is the chronic patient between medical crises. In an endless circular pattern he alternates between community and the institutions. His building is the central concern of the local police precinct. His petty crimes and misdemeanors involve the major part of court personnel's time. Typically, he goes to the hospital in an ambulance to die after untreated illness. Thus his characteristic relationship is chiefly to the municipal services at times of crisis or emergency.

As for the individual person residing in such an environment, there is little to nourish hope of change. The sick remain sick; the unemployed remain unemployed. These SROs are homes where material deprivation and chronic crises breed an environment which reinforces its own pathology.

The destitute people described in this book are an amalgam; they are not one ethnic group; they are not poor because of a single common economic or social cause; nor are they a cluster of the aging poor such as are found in nursing homes, or Skid Row derelicts brought together by alcohol and geography. The unifying thread of their lives is their common home in the SRO, an island of poverty and dilapidation, surrounded by the middle class. The tenants are defined by their neighbors, and define themselves, as different. They become an enclave, ignored and ostracized as long as they remain invisible, threatened and ultimately removed when their stress spills into the street in the form of fighting, muggings, and drunken loitering.

Despite this bleak demographic picture, a more intimate encounter with SRO tenants reveals a way of life with undergirdings of strength and self-protection despite their double burdens of social and physical handicaps. A mutual aid system functions, though somewhat haphazardly, for most tenants, and their relationships have vivid and pleasurable aspects intertwined with the destructive ones. The tapestry of this way of life is delineated in Chapter 1. Chapters 2 through 8 describe the development of a helping process within the buildings. Our initial intrusion as social workers into the SRO world was a naïve response to community anxiety and anger; we approached the mandate to "do something" with skepticism, distaste and fear. Our understanding and appreciation of the way of life in SROs developed gradually as we attempted to become helpful. The more useful forms of this help were largely dictated by the social system and its norms and values as they were unfolded to us. Thus these chapters detail the process of interdigitation between tenants and ourselves as we searched for congruence between the form of help we could give and they could use. The programs which developed, for all the misinformation and misunderstanding which marked their growth, had far more effect on both the internal life of the buildings and their exterior visibility than expected. Chapters 7 and 8 present an analysis of some subsystems in the SRO, inferences as to why the programs achieved their impact, and recommendations for softening and stabilizing the lives of those destined to remain within the web of the SRO. An appendix reviews the historical development of the SRO in New York City.

COMMUNITIES OF THE ALONE

SRO as a Village Community

1

> Is not the kindred of a common fate a closer tie than that of birth?
>
> —NATHANIEL HAWTHORNE, *The Ambitious Guest*

The "problem" SROs which shall be our concern are those in which three different elements coalesce: a deteriorating building, inadequate management, and socially or physically sick tenants. Each of these reinforces, balances, and shapes the others.

Each building has a "personality," developed from a combination of the particular personality characteristics of the manager, his intake and exclusion policies, and the characteristics of the dominant cluster of his long-term residents. Such "building personalities" are well-known to the great majority of SRO dwellers and each can be described quite specifically in terms of the people living in it. One such building may be widely known to accept alcoholics but not addicts; another, elderly people; a third, homosexuals. Some are "wide open," in that the manager accepts all comers at any hour to fill his building, taking the calculated risk of destruction of property. At the other extreme are tight, homogeneous, relatively stable groups of long-term residents of a specific ethnic group or class. The vast majority of SROs fall between these extremes; a mixture of pathologies, ages and ethnicities which emerge as a recognizable blend.

Nine SROs studied in detail reveal very similar configurations. There are few young people, most are forty and older; there are whites, Puerto Ricans and Negroes, the particular mix depending on the intake policy of the manager. A small majority are Negroes from the rural South. At least three-quarters of the population have major chronic health problems such as tuberculosis, heart disease, kidney disease, diabetes, cirrhosis of the liver, and blindness. Superimposed are social and mental problems, the most conspicuous of which is alcoholism. In some buildings, well over half the tenants are alcoholics. Two much smaller groups in many of the buildings are addicts and those with obvious mental illness. The men usually outnumber the women two-to-one. Fifty percent or more are welfare recipients; much of the rest of the population is employed sporadically and in unskilled jobs.

The residents along one corridor in one of the buildings are representative:

A twenty-eight-year-old Negro man, who is the superintendent of the building and an extremely effective handyman, lost half of one hand in an industrial accident; he is entirely illiterate, and under treatment for V.D.

A middle-aged Negro woman with V.D. who is supported by the superintendent.

A Puerto Rican man, sixty-two years old, tiny, emaciated and actively hallucinating; younger "friends" use his room for alcoholic parties and impromptu all-night drumming sessions. He rarely leaves his room. He is a Department of Welfare client.

A sixty-five-year-old Southern Negro woman who has arthritis and severe edema of both legs; walking is difficult for her. She has no confidence in doctors and sends to the South for herbs for her illness. She is a Department of Welfare client.

A middle-aged Negro woman who is totally blind and an occasional heavy drinker; she is a Department of Welfare client.

A forty-five-year-old Puerto Rican woman who is a full-time laundry worker; she keeps her room in extreme disorder. The landlord considers her mentally retarded.

A forty-seven-year-old Negro man who is an alcoholic and has lived there for four years; he has a chronic heart condition caused by untreated rheumatic heart disease contracted as a child. He is a Department of Welfare client.

Normal bridges of communication between the outer world and SRO buildings are weak. There are usually no telephones other than a lobby pay booth, often out of order; mailboxes are routinely empty. Among SRO tenants ties to primary family tend to be absent or are tenuous. Most do not vote, nor do they belong to voluntary groups such as churches or clubs. The extremely negative attitudes of their neighbors are well known to them. Most tenants anticipate and experience rejecting, humiliating or depersonalizing responses on the part of many community institutions, such as police, hospitals and social agencies, to their requests. These limiting social experiences reinforce their tendencies toward self-isolation. Characteristically, outsiders find tenants either apathetic or passively watchful, masking shame, fear and underlying anger.

In the midst of this grim misery, a new and unexpected discovery was made. In these walled-off villages for society's rejects, we found a complex and profoundly social community. Somehow a way of life has developed in the buildings to cope, however ineffectively, with the endemic illness, pain, fear and hunger. People in the buildings, more often than not, have friends there; there are spokesmen and protectors of those less able, mediators with the manager, some who cook for others and some who are dependent on others to care for them.

The lives of all but a few of the tenants are actively intertwined, a finding which sharply contradicts the stereotype of the single, unattached individual as reclusive (22) (25) (34). Some recurrent patterns of relationships are the well-defined matriarchal quasi-family, the all-male drinking clique, the long-term lesbian pair, the addicted prostitute with one or more male addicts whom she supports. These networks produce an informal system of mutual help. For example, an older woman, a welfare recipient, considers it her task to care for certain bedridden residents. She cleans, cooks for, and feeds them on a fairly regular basis, for which she receives no compensation other than status. A young man who has a substantial supply of tranquilizers does not use these drugs himself; instead, he dispenses them, one by one, to people in trouble who come to talk to him. A strong former boxer is called upon to stop dangerous fights. A woman who looks after seven alcoholic men keeps a jar of cigarette butts, which she has collected, for anyone who needs them.

Alcoholism is the predominant social problem among SRO

tenants. In the nine buildings, 50 to 90 percent of tenants fit this description; in all, between 500 and 600 individuals. Drinking serves may functions. For the solitary person it relieves loneliness; for social cliques it is the paramount shared activity from which all other collective activities radiate. For every alcoholic it is a defense against physical pain, anxiety, and depression. Dependence on it has been expressed often by SRO tenants: "Without it I couldn't stand my life or myself," or, "At least there is a little hope in that red bottle."

The majority of SRO alcoholics are Negro, male, and over forty. There is also a minority group of Negro women alcoholics and a much smaller but highly visible group of white alcoholics. But the SRO alcoholics appear not to be equivalent to today's Skid Rowers moved uptown. Very few SRO drinkers, to our knowledge, had ever lived on the Bowery. Some had ended up in the Bowery men's shelter during a binge but quickly returned to an SRO. The tenants separate themselves from the "Bowery bums" as being a social cut above them. Men on the Bowery also define the SRO dweller as socially superior.

There are three social patterns which are quite distinct among SRO alcoholics: 1) the alcoholic "family," usually dominated by a middle-aged Negro matriarch; 2) the small all-male "bottle gang" group; 3) the solitary drinkers. Usually the first and second groups continuously tipple wine, bought and shared as a group. Except at times of special stress, these alcoholics do not appear grossly drunk, nor are they incoherent, though they may become high, loud, and disruptive. The third type, the solitary drinkers, resemble the addicted alcoholic in that they drink until they are stuporous, then dry out and repeat this pattern with varying lengths of time between binges. They do not treat others and usually do not have the social relationships which would make bottle-sharing feasible. These drinkers prefer hard liquor to wine if they can afford it.

The most common constellation is the matriarchal quasi-family, in which the dominant woman tends to feed, protect, punish, and set norms for the alcoholic "family" members. They share some meals, and the room of the leader is a hub of continuous social activity. The women are usually called "Mom" or "Momma" and other members of the group also have kinship names: "Brother," "Uncle," "Grandma," and "Baby." The members tend to be middle-aged, physically sick, and more psychologically dependent. Sometimes nonalcoholic, mentally ill people or retarded individuals attach themselves to these families and are cared for in them. The matriarch, herself usually an alcoholic, has much power to dictate both the behavior of the family members and their relationships to each other. Such a family of four elderly men and their "mother" came regularly to meetings of the tenants' organization. She functioned as a disciplining but loving parent as she sat with a belt or piece of rope among her "family." If one of them became boisterous, she put her arms around his shoulders and simultaneously belted him across the legs. Over a dozen such alcoholic women were located as the heads of well-defined families in the project buildings.

The second type, the peer drinkers, appears to be made up of younger men who are sporadically employed; they play cards together, have parties and sometimes share a woman. They are similar to the Skid Row "bottle gang" in that, among them, almost no drinking takes place alone. Bottle gangs (31) are formed routinely with a fairly stable membership in which all contribute whatever money they have or can panhandle, and the whole group buys a bottle and shares equally regardless of the proportion of the initial investment of the individual. Those who attempt to drink more than their share are ostracized.

But, in contrast to the Skid Row alcoholics who bottle-gang in bars, SRO alcoholics usually drink in someone's room. Not only is wine by the glass too expensive but the bottle gang pattern cannot be enacted in the uptown bars. A scene re-created in every SRO is the peer drinking group gathered to split a bottle or two. The group sits close together on the bed or the floor and passes the wine from mouth to mouth until it is gone. A warm, teasing, intimate buzz can be heard down the long corridor. There is almost never a dispute about amounts of drink; fair sharing is assumed, as is a fair division or provision of wine. The daily drinker consumes wine from two to four pints a day at 51 cents a pint, the cheapest domestic type available. He is slightly "lit" but neither incoherent nor uncoordinated. When more money is available on check day, he may drink more; that day and the next are a time of retreat from usual social behavior into the bottle, but always on a shared basis.

Wine is also used as a barter item and as a gift for favors or services rendered. Someone shopping for another may be paid with extra money for wine. An unexpected windfall, a clothing check from the Department of Social Services (D.S.S.), or a successful pickpocketing enterprise means a party for the "in" group. An extension of this social scene takes place on the stoop or along the railings outside the building where a group of four or five men will pass around a bottle of wine concealed in a paper bag.

Attitudes toward alcoholism by alcoholics vary. Predictably there is some desire to conceal and deny the problem to outsiders. However, within the building and especially within the drinking group, there is a strong acceptance and defense of it, despite fear of the violence which certain solitary alcoholics display. A very few of these alcoholics brawl, throw bottles and garbage out of windows, break in doors and windows when they are very drunk. Others in the building make some effort to control these individuals.

Lastly, we come to the solitary drinker—the truly addicted alcoholic who lives from binge to binge; he tends to be a lonely soul, a source of pity and shame to other tenants. Never part of a family or bottle gang, he drinks in his room or is found stoned in the hall or in the street. Other tenants will usually bring him home to the SRO rather than let him be picked up by the police. In one instance, a fellow tenant went to the men's shelter looking for such a tenant, though the alcoholic was no one's "friend."

All but a few solitary drinkers are white, of Irish or Italian descent; there are also a handful of Jews and Orientals. The lone drinkers are in far deeper psychological trouble than the Negro alcoholics. They are hostile to help from any source, bitter and antisocial, and are committing slow suicide. Among them are those who are near death from cirrhosis and severe malnutrition.

The other alcoholics are extremely solicitous of them. Some are cared for and nursed. In two buildings, DT's were recognized and treated by giving the sick tenant wine. In one building a woman always had a pint on hand for this specific purpose. There was wide recognition that hospitalization, even if it were available, was likely to be futile, for few hospitals eagerly admit a moribund elderly alcoholic with other multiple physical problems.

The addicts also know one another well and tend to develop pairs or triangular relationships. However, they move from one SRO to another more frequently than alcoholics because of surveillance and narcotic raids. Usually alcoholics and addicts mutually exclude one another. Very few tenants, mostly elderly whites, remain truly isolated.

Every building has a number of tenants whom the majority recognizes as outsiders, different from themselves, thus marginal even to the SRO world. These are working people and the few successful members of the cool criminal world who are respected but feared, and who usually hold high status.

On the other hand, the lesbian pairs and triangles, the elderly white men and women who have become recluses or hoarders, and the buildings' news carriers and gossips who are socially marginal to all groups are seen as low-status tenants by the majority.

In every building, there are lesbian triangles. These women are usually Negro alcoholics and among some of them much violent fighting occurs, subsiding as quickly as it arises and apparently forgotten by the contestants, despite cuts and black eyes. The fighting usually happens when one partner, out of favor for the moment, becomes jealously enraged while she is drunk. Three lesbian pairs had settled permanent relationships of many years' duration; they were all involved in programs and produced important leadership.

In almost every building there were men who were chronically preyed upon: their money and things "borrowed" or stolen, their possessions taken, or their rooms used as gathering places for other socially stronger tenants. A few such victims felt

helpless and afraid, but most found satisfaction in their relationship to the preyers, upon whom they really depended. For
example, a mentally defective white man permitted the use of
his room for frequent bongo drum parties lasting most of the
night, much to the despair of other tenants, the manager, and
the block. He would remain quietly on the periphery as he
watched the black musicians and smiled vacantly and beat time
gently on the wall. Periodically, they sent him out for wine,
which he eagerly bought for them with his own meager money.
He did not drink himself. When the wine was all gone, or the
insistent complaints about the noise became threatening, his
"friends" would melt away, his room a shambles, his food
money for the week spent, and his neighbors furious.

How does it happen that tenants on the top floor know that
the investigator or policeman is walking toward the building?
The network of newsrunners is infallible. It appears to operate
generally like this:

In almost every building there are tenants, usually women,
who watch and report. They have lived in the building a long
time but do not have firm connections with any social group
there. They stand endlessly and patiently by the entrance or sit
watching the street from their windows. They know faces, names,
relationships, and store the minor dramas they see for their
pleasure and future gossip. They are the first to know of a
change in homosexual partners, the case closed by Welfare, the
manager's intention to evict someone. Three of these self-
appointed communication links were elderly Jewish women,
"yentehs," who were isolated socially in the building, but whose
gossip function was used and appreciated. Belonging to no
group, they connected in this way all the subgroups. The manager's tenant-desk clerks also had a similar role in linking
managers and tenants, and in creating a sense of a unified community of known individuals. They too were marginal to all
groups.

The social groups are racially mixed. Color prejudice is a
minor divisive force as compared to differences of class and
pathology. As self-help programs developed and ingroup feel-

ings were strengthened, racial prejudice emerged—a luxury possible only when fear, hunger and pain have been abated. Tolerance flourishes at the bottom of the barrel.

The members of these friendship groups give mutual support to each other's deviant or maladaptive behavior, but they also provide the human association, the sense of some help and belonging that makes physical survival possible and emotional life meaningful.

We found the SRO culture to be sensory, immediate, spontaneous, auditory, and action-oriented as opposed to logical, reflective, visual. Communication favors the nonverbal over the verbal. Vocabularies are small, abstractions and generalizations few; the concrete, the personal, and the present are more characteristic of conversational content than the general, causal, or consequential. Nonverbal communication reflects with dramatic vividness the precise state of individuals and the quality of their connectedness to others at the moment. Tenants habitually use touch to communicate feeling. A hand on a shoulder can discipline, constrain, encourage, admire, love, seduce, or frighten. Gesture, posture and facial expression, too, convey vivid messages.

People permit and feel comfortable with closer body proximity than would be habitual among the middle class. Six people crowding onto a couch, lap-sitting, leaning, hair tousling, and hugging frequently occur between people who are on only mildly friendly terms. Sexual aggressiveness is inconspicuous and what appears to be seductive or lewd acting-out often seems more related to a childlike need for body contact and nearness.

Names in the SRO world reflect the self-image of its tenants. For those with complicated past lives, many marriages, arrests, multiple homes or children, last names are flexible floating labels, several of which apply. This looseness creates confusion in D.S.S., hospital records, and the manager's list of occupants; mother and son may go by different last names; one tenant has two differently labeled hospital records. It reflects, for some, a desire to be invisible, elusive; for others, it once again points to a person who feels himself to be without history or future, whose identity in the outer world is insignificant.

First names and/or nicknames are more fixed. Names such as Candy, Mug, Tank, Champ, Tango, Lucky, Squeeze, Flash, Six-Six, and Flick accurately describe the person both affectionately and in symbolic language. Other names indicate distance: Miss Bingo, The Knitting Man, The Cat Lady. There are intimate child-names like Billy-Billy, Daisyette and Baby-Josie. Many names of women are neuter: Mickey, Sandy, Frankie and Jackie. Generally people are called by their first names unless they are marginal, disliked loners or those who carry a kind of dignity and respect that demands a Mr. or Mrs. or simple last name—"Springfield," "Dunston." Lastly, every building has several "Mommas" or "Grandmas," many of whom occupy positions of prestige. "Pop" tends to be a term of faint derision or pity and is given to very old men.

Relationships among tenants are characterized by a wide spectrum of acted-out feelings, punctuated by minor short-lived crises. Tenants are at times generous and loyal to one another in situations demanding considerable sacrifice. For example, a $45 fund was collected in one building from 21 tenants, the superintendent and some of the maintenance staff to prevent the burying of a tenant in Potter's Field. There are also regular eruptions of physical fighting. The violence of these outbursts is soon forgotten by participants and bystanders alike. This type of antisocial behavior often seems to be in response to pent-up emotions, dammed behind a wall of loneliness, boredom, hunger, rage and frustration. This may be enacted within the buildings in the form of fistfights, knife slashings, brawls, broken windows, binges, and retreats into psychotic episodes. The rhythm of life is no different for the SRO group than for any other unemployed and bored lower-class group where a flat psychosocial landscape is punctuated by seeking or creating excitement and thrills. A few individuals in the SRO population with poorest impulse control create the "action" and become conspicuous to the community, giving the building its reputation. The remaining majority respond with passivity and depression, experiencing the uproar vicariously.

Another form of violence having different causes and involving different personality types also exists. This has an economic function designed to maintain income or an addicted habit. Its intent is neither excitement nor hurt, but gain. The violence is acted out in the form of mugging, purse-snatching and theft, usually on the surrounding middle-class population, but occasionally on another SRO dweller. However, there is a widespread norm, to which all but a very few disturbed sociopathic individuals conform, which forbids preying on the people who live in one's own SRO. The violence of either type, however important to the community, must be viewed only as a symptom, or benchmark, of intense individual and group suffering.

The higher one's social class, the more extensive one's typical life space—that is, the geographical boundaries within which one operates and feels comfortable. At the bottom of the social scale, the SRO tenants have profoundly restricted their life space. Habitually the tenants stay within a two-block radius of the building, many tenants spending days on end without going outside. Some do not know how to use the bus or subway system and feel incapable of traveling alone to distant parts of the city. A trip to a clinic might be a major anxiety-provoking event. They buy in specific stores in the immediate neighborhood which are known to be friendly. Nearby parks are sometimes viewed as territories of middle-class mothers, and the disreputable-looking tenants tend to be harassed by police. A favorite place of many are the benches lining the parks or on the traffic islands in the middle of major avenues. For specific tenants, these last are outdoor living rooms; the same spot on the same bench is occupied daily by each tenant "to watch the people go by" and "catch some air."

Space in the buildings is used more freely. Most tenants have friends and may venture on some other floors and move around in the building. Strangers on a floor are quickly noted and watched. Stokes (28), in her sociometric study of one building, notes that proximity favors the creation of friendships on one's own corridor first and on one's own floor, second. However, over half of the friendships developed between tenants on different floors. Since managers usually assign common pathologies to each floor, the addicts, alcoholics and the working people tend to know one another first and best. A very few tenants are frightened and truly isolated. There are recluses who also scurry in and out of the building furtively, hoping to be seen by no one. One elderly and timid white woman timed an anxious trip to the bathroom when other tenants on her floor were out or asleep and paid a cleaning woman to shop for her. She would speak to no one and let her investigator from D.S.S. in only after positive assurance that it was she.

Current time, subjectively perceived, has—like music—rate, rhythm, intensity and mood. The SRO dweller, excluding the addicts, experiences time as a vast, formless present; the hours, days, months and seasons have only a shadowy impact on his monotonous, floating sense of apathy, of existing and waiting for nothing at all. The few patterned activities, the mild punctuations, are the arrival of his rent money, his two meals, his easy socializing, and his bottles. There is little impetus to go out, fix his room, read, or write a letter. Clocks and watches are scarce. An event of any kind is savored and treasured: He must not fix his dinner now, even though he is hungry, because then the evening will be too long and empty. He needs to speak to the manager about the lock on his door not working, but he'll do that tomorrow, since today he is sharing a pint with a friend down the hall. One minor event thus fills the day.

Orwell (20) connects time and poverty as follows:

For, when you are approaching poverty, you make one discovery which outweighs some of the others. You discover boredom and mean complications and beginnings of hunger, but you also discover the great redeeming feature of poverty: the fact that it annihilates the future. Within certain limits, it is actually true that the less money you have, the less you worry. When you have a hundred francs in the world, you are liable to the most craven panics. When you have only three francs, you are quite indifferent; for three francs will feed you till tomorrow, and you cannot think further than that.

You are bored, but you are not afraid. You think vaguely, "I shall be starving in a day or two—shocking, isn't it?" And then the mind wanders to other topics. A bread and margarine diet does, to some extent, provide its own anodyne (p. 16).

The past is best not remembered. Dates, names and places are vague; sequences of jobs, illnesses, and time served in jail are remembered without color of specificity. Past experiences are rarely used as connecting links to others, such as "Once I was . . ." or "Yes, that happened to me, too." For some, facts are easily fused with fantasy and the same event retold is unrecognized but not uninteresting. Friendship shared deeply at the moment is fragile and fleeting over time; possessions, too, are few, and, with the exception of the burrowing collectors, or downwardly mobile elderly people—holding onto a more benign past in objects, pictures, a suitcase, or a madonna—expendable. Moving is a simple matter for most—two or three cartons, a radio, a few pots, and a one-burner electric hot plate.

And what of the future? Its formlessness, the absence of hope or change in it, sets the mood from which apathy about appearance or medical care grows. An old man said to a worker, "Why should I go to the hospital? They will only keep me to die."

For the SRO tenant on welfare, the weeks are patterned in cycles of the "check days"; welfare checks arrive on the 1st and 15th of each month. These mild peaks of excitement begin as the self-appointed lobby-sitters wait for the mail. As it is sorted by the manager, tenants drift into the lobby and form a loose line. Since, from time to time—and unexpectedly—someone's check does not arrive, there is an edge of anxiety. Its absence can be catastrophic, entailing an emergency call to the welfare center. The manager may be tolerant and wait to be paid his rent for the next two weeks, or he may use this as an excuse to evict an undesirable tenant. The manager has no way of checking the reason for the delay: perhaps it *is* only a delay; perhaps the tenant has been cut off, and the manager will never get his money back. In socially friendly buildings, people chat, joke, and some compare checks. In the one building where people are strangers

to one another, there is a furtive, silent distance as each slips
back to his room with the remainder of his money in cash. Then
begins the exodus: to shop, to pay back endless minor debts,
and to return laden with food, or bottles or bags. This is the day
of binges for some, a renewal of hope in storing food, a day for
buying a carefully saved-for bottle of shampoo or aspirin, for
getting Japanese rubber sandals or cheap sneakers for under a
dollar at the local discount store. Shoes, overcoats and underwear
are chronically needed. Stockings, underwear, brassieres, rub-
bers, raincoats, and dress clothes are luxuries.

This is also the day when those who prey from outside the
building slowly cruise the corridors trying to roll an alcoholic,
pick up a radio or jacket in a room left open by the unwary. It
is a day of eruptions of violence and fights with managers. During the ensuing fourteen days, the buildings become more and
more quiet and the last few days are times of hunger and despair,
as money has been used up, wisely and unwisely, and there is no
alternative but to wait. Thus the pace is slow, the rhythm marked
in two-week cycles, the intensity linked to the rhythm, and the
mood deeply depressed.

A worker commented on the check-day lobby scene:

Watching the people come down, I had the feeling that this was
no monastery, but a Catholic hospital, in which the piped-in Rosary
every night added to the prevailing sense of doom and imminent
death. All but perhaps three young men, who appeared to be quite
hale and hearty, had obvious physical illness or injuries, from severe
eye trouble corrected or not, twisted spines, limps, terrible coughs,
obesity, terrible skinniness, just about everything a person could
have and still get down to get one's check.

The quality of silence was oppressive—not only was it unusual
to me to see five to ten people in the small, physical area of the
lobby with such noiselessness, but I felt that something was sucking
up all the sound, like some kind of very active sound-proofing. This
is the kind of feeling I can see in the manager's face sometimes; not
actually a tightness, which makes hard lines, but a withdrawal away-
from feeling.

The silence got to me, and though I had intended to try to open
conversations for almost half the time I was there, I was stonily

silent, too. Then at one point, the people were gone, and I asked the manager if it was always that quiet, to which he said that he "makes all the noise around here," and laughed.

Shopping and food preparation is a major activity, fraught with frustration beyond the lack of money. Every six to seven rooms on each corridor share a bath and kitchen. Basic maintenance of these shabby facilities is grossly lacking. Leaks, nonfunctioning stoves and refrigerators, and the absence of water valves are common. Where no responsibility is assigned, any degree of cleanliness is hard to come by, and most users are too ill and indifferent to take responsibility. Some kitchens are scarcely used at all; others are regularly used by the same people. As a substitute, a great many tenants have hot plates in their rooms, a minor illegality almost never stopped by the manager.

The tenants receiving welfare average, after rent is deducted, a basic weekly allowance of $15 for food, toilet articles, minor clothing, travel and laundry. Some tenants have additional allowances for special foods, medication and other items. A very few tenants receive additional amounts to enable them to use restaurants. A restaurant allowance is difficult to obtain and seriously disabled tenants who cannot easily shop for themselves either struggle out periodically or ask neighbors to shop for them—sometimes for a fee or a pint bottle of the cheapest wine.

Usually two meals a day are prepared, a very late breakfast and supper. Meat, milk, cheese, fresh fruits, and vegetables are conspicuously absent in these meals. A heavy emphasis on cereals, bread, rice, cornmeal, canned tuna, spaghetti, peanut butter and jelly is evident. Cold cuts are very popular, as are pork products. Since refrigerators are dirty and stored food is stolen (a chronic complaint), shopping from meal to meal is necessary—an expensive and time-consuming pattern. Milk and perishables are kept on windowsills. Some tenants make an elaborate production of meal preparation, using it as the high point of a long and empty day. But most are casual—an opened can of spaghetti or soup is put in a pot of boiling water, then eaten out of the can with a plastic spoon. This is the whole of dinner.

A day curiously marked for the alcoholic is Sunday—a day when liquor stores are closed. In nearly every building, some enterprising tenant-operator has foreseen the business possibilities in this situation and stocks up on wine to be sold on Sunday at a 200 or 300 percent markup, or on credit at the same rate. Most alcoholics somehow do not plan ahead for Sunday and are "taken" every time.

A second time cycle, minor but perceptible in the life of the building, is the seven-day cycle ending Friday night for those who work. These people represent 10 to 20 percent of the population in the buildings. They are gone all day, complain of noise from the late-reveling welfare tenants and shun their activities. They party among themselves or outside the building on Friday nights and sleep on the weekends. The season holidays, Thanksgiving, Christmas and Easter, are times of special pain when the tenants try to make up for their lost families, some by drawing closer to one another, others by retreating into the bottle.

Altering this dull routine with little stimulation are the unexpected events: a death, an occasional murder or suicide. These are experienced vicariously; rumor flies, witnesses are rapidly listened to. The fear itself, or the injury to some tenant, is compensated for by the renewed sense of excitement and of life which it engenders. Gorky (5) observed the same phenomenon nearly 100 years ago:

> Long afterwards I understood that to Russians, through the poverty and squalor of their lives, suffering comes as a diversion, is turned into a game and they play at it like children and rarely feel ashamed of their misfortune. In the monotony of everyday existence, grief comes as a holiday, and a fire is an entertainment. A scratch embellishes an empty face (p. 172).

While vicarious excitement is actively enjoyed, expanded, told and retold, some exceptional events make no perceptible impact. The riots that took place in Harlem in the summer of 1964 barely troubled the tenants in a building who were in fact only a dozen blocks away. Most seemed uninformed and disinterested in news of all kinds. Newspapers were seldom read, and events in the outside world were unknown. The riots were shrugged off with the general attitude among blacks and whites alike that they had enough troubles of their own.

Similarly, in another building an unknown man was found murdered in the basement. There was mild interest, some gawking as the police came, and some speculation as to who and why. But the injury or death of a known person creates excitement, anxiety, buzz and whispering in the halls and rooms for days.

Most managers have long since ceased to rely on police protection. Policemen cannot enter a building unless an assault is being enacted and there are witnesses, and most tenants are afraid to be witnesses against one another. One manager reported that he is regularly shaken down by local policemen. Some managers create their own internal police system; others accept violence, knife fights, bottle-throwing, etc., as a part of the way the population lives and make little effort to control it. Some evict aggressive and violent tenants without hesitation; others wish they could but fear reprisals from tenants. Managers are sometimes physically attacked by tenants; one was punched, another knocked out when intercepting a fight. The manager in one building was murdered at his desk; a second was shot and robbed after a scuffle.

The managers usually strike up some kind of a bargaining relationship with the dominant tenants in each building. Sometimes these leaders develop an uneasy alliance with the managers, who recognize their value as economic assets. Because of them, there is less property damage, less public disturbance, and a turnover reduction. In emergencies such as illness, death, robbery, fire, or psychiatric crises, they sometimes work as a team. Several managers avoid handling such crises, leaving the tenants themselves to negotiate with the outside institutions.

Mrs. J. often determines the need for an ambulance and asks the manager to call the hospital. Then she accompanies the sick tenant as he goes from hospital to hospital, state hospital, or prison. She pleads with the manager to hold his welfare check until he returns, when she welcomes him back "home."

Mrs. C. and the manager have a furiously affectionate relationship. They are either shouting at each other or not speaking. He needs her to do his job but is jealous of her power and the tenants' attachment to her. Sporadically, he offers free soda or gives small amounts of money to tenants. At others times, he is quite punitive, threatening to evict a tenant for rent unpaid or a noisy night. The leader usually intervenes and persuades the manager to give the tenant "one more chance."

There are ritual enactments between certain tenants and managers; e.g., the manager threatens to throw somebody out and the person begs to be reinstated. This pattern has a repetitive artificial quality as the person continues to live in the building, and the manager continues to threaten month after month. In a reverse pattern, a group of tenants recurrently baited a manager into impotent rage for their own amusement.

Lack of emotional control leading to the expression of explosive anger appears to be characteristic of both tenants and managers. It is as though the tenants call forth this response from men already poorly defended against their own impulses. As a system, the SRO sanctions emotionally erratic behavior by the tenants, and elicits similar behavior from the manager.

Managers and tenants thus become locked into a common reciprocal relationship characterized by mutual dependence. Each is tied to the other by far more than the real exchange of money for housing. Subtle congruent needs produce a meshing which sometimes is beneficial to both, but which may also reinforce the problems of both.

The tenants' and managers' isolation is symbolized by the ostracism of their buildings by the neighborhood; in addition, the absence of ordinary maintenance services, switchboard, pay telephones, working door locks or even mirrors, speaks of a profound dehumanization of the tenants. The managers are under no compulsion to provide the usual amenities: sheets, housekeeping services, clean elevators in operating order, a lobby for meeting friends, or protection from vagrants. They struggle between two conflicting ends: to preserve their property against violent tenants who kick in doors, destroy furniture, and are a source of police calls, and to hold onto as many of these tenants as possible. The economic survival of the managers depends on a steady flow of new D.S.S. clients to fill vacancies, on minimizing property damage, and on avoiding enforcement of building codes.

The managers are either partial or sole owners in all but two of the buildings. (Those two are owned by syndicates which employ the managers who return a certain percentage to the syndicates on a monthly basis, but who otherwise function autonomously.)

The typical manager runs his operation from 9:00 A.M. to 7:00 P.M. from a tiny, grill-windowed office. Here, twice a month, he cashes tenants' welfare checks, withholding the rent and any loans, and returning the remainder. His office is his fortress and his retreat; more often than not, the door between the dilapidated lobby and the office is locked. Weekly rentals average $15 per person, about $65 per month. By comparison, rentals for 1½ room efficiency apartments in low-income Housing Authority projects range from $30 to $50 a month.

Because the tenant has no options in finding alternate housing, the manager gives the tenant a service in harboring him at all, in tolerating his binges, in concealing his petty vices, in delaying his institutionalization as he becomes senile or psychotic, and in shielding him from being shamed by the outside world.

Eight of the nine SRO managers we have come to know are remarkably similar in background. All but one are aging Jewish refugees who came to the United States during or after World War II; seven are survivors of concentration camps. They are now married, have children, and live in lower-middle-class suburbs. Most have serious physical disabilities such as heart disease, deafness, ulcerative colitis, or liver disease.

One encompassing characteristic of the managers is recurring ambivalence about their work and about tenants. On the one hand, they may exhibit varying degrees of despotism and overt cruelty; on the other, they partly fear, partly pity tenants and may show this in their attempts to please them and to be helpful to those in pain and crises. Like the protagonist of *The Pawnbroker,* the managers are, at times, harsh and depriving; at other times, openly or secretly protective, generous and kindly.

This ambivalence creates inconsistency of behavior in all phases of their relationships and their functioning as managers, including their characteristic ways of handling intake, eviction, deviance, violence, crises, and the external institutions impinging on the building, such as the D.S.S. and the hospital.

Among the tenants, the counterpart of this managerial ambivalence is the oscillation between fear of the manager and a subtle understanding of him and his needs. The fear produces rebellion, taunting, scapegoating, and avoidance of the manager, while the recognition of their mutual dependency produces begging, doing favors, "behaving," tattling on others, and exaggeration and dramatization of difficulty or pain to elicit a helpful response. Managers who call an ambulance or the police are relied upon by the tenants and receive grudging admiration and affection for this.

Each manager has both a stated and an actual policy as gatekeeper of his building. Some insist that they do not accept drug addicts, alcoholics, people from mental institutions, welfare tenants, Negroes, the elderly, the crippled, or some other category of population. Yet most of the managers develop heterogeneous tenant populations. Some do not screen tenants at all; others screen out those who are not docile enough in the intake interview.

Managers protect tenants in certain areas. Managers' attitudes of benevolent laissez-faire allow for a whole series of illegal activities, such as reselling wine on credit and at a higher price to alcoholics, peddling narcotics, "shooting galleries" (group gatherings for the purpose of taking drugs), and prostitution, provided that the activity is not too flagrant or observable. Further, these managers rarely evict anyone, with the exception of those tenants, usually women, who are chronic active instigators of violence.

The tenants need the controls which some managers exert:

A mentally retarded alcoholic, who was relocated into one building, had habitually urinated in the elevator of the previous SRO where he had lived. He continued this after relocation. The manager quietly became friendly with him, visited him in his room and then on the third day told him firmly and kindly that he must use the toilet. The man did not even know where the bathroom was, and the manager took him there, flushed the toilet, showed him how to lock and unlock the door. The elevator was urine-free from that time on.

In *Beyond the Melting Pot,* Glazer and Moynihan (4) point out:

The problem of creating a community is an enormous task, and it may seem unfair to demand of a landlord that he undertake this task. . . . The improvement of the [N. Y. City Housing Authority] projects as communities probably depends on a host of measures that are even more difficult than affecting their racial composition: involving the people of the projects in their management and maintenance, encouraging and strengthening forms of organization among them (even when the main purpose of these organizations seems to be to attack the management), encouraging forms of self-help in them, varying their population, occupationally as well as racially by greater tolerance in admissions, reducing the stark difference of the projects from their surroundings by changing their appearance, considering more seriously the impact of their design on the social life that they enfold, all this and more have been suggested. . . .

These requirements are far heavier in the marginal SROs, which are communities on the edge of disequilibrium. The managers of these SROs are constantly under stress. They consider themselves real estate businessmen, but they are in reality untrained directors of staffless institutions. To house and adequately care for their tenants, they would need internal police protection, medical and nursing services, recreation and social services. The inconsistent, tempestuous, and, at times, inept behavior we have described may be seen as frustrated and angry reactions to an impossible occupational task.

Since the majority of tenants are welfare recipients, the managers' primary source of income is from rents paid by the Department of Social Services in New York. Thus the D.S.S. is the unwilling economic backbone of SROs. There simply is no alternative housing available to its single clients. A series of discriminatory practices in public and private housing severely

limit choices for "undesirable" people. Public housing regulations specify twenty-one personal characteristics which are
considered disqualifying. SRO tenants rarely are acceptable.

The twin American creeds, the virtue of work and the limitless
opportunity of the individual to succeed, profoundly influence
current attitudes toward welfare grants. At this time, welfare support is conceived as residual services to citizens whose normal
productivity has been interrupted temporarily. Chronic welfare
recipients—such as those in SROs—the aged, the mentally ill,
the blind, the permanently ill or disabled receive welfare payments, but, as it were, grudgingly. Alcoholics and addicts are in
an uncomfortable no-man's-land, since in theory they have the
capacity to be self-supporting because they are neither recognized to be physically ill nor do they have histories of hospitalization for mental illness.

Until very recently, the welfare worker was required to supervise the management of his client-ward's budget and check on
his employability. At the same time he was expected to establish
a relationship of trust, respect and confidentiality. This inconsistency has burdened the welfare worker's functioning as the
sole legally mandated helping agent for the SRO dweller. In
1962 in New York City, income maintenance was separated
from social services performed by the Department of Social
Services. Beginning in 1964, the welfare center which serves the
great majority of West Side SROs, the Amsterdam Social Service
Center, initiated important changes in services to SRO clients.
Case loads in SROs were consolidated so that most welfare
recipients in one building would have a single investigator. Since
then the D.S.S. has gradually taken over the entire responsibility
for both work with groups and individuals in many SRO buildings (15) (16) (33). One unit has as its entire case load the welfare recipients of three project buildings, and its workers have
become part of the daily life of the tenants.

The nearly closed SRO system is a private poorhouse supported by public funds, without public accountability. Though
marginal by usual standards, it serves the function for society of
providing housing for single individuals of the city who can

neither function more autonomously as productive citizens nor maintain their existing meager level of functioning upon institutionalization. The SRO way of life, however, affords them an unexpected network of social supports which evolves from within the SRO system itself.

2

The Entry Phase

> If you treat an individual as he is, he will stay as he is, but
> if you treat him as if he were what he ought to be and could be,
> he will become what he ought to be and could be.
>
> —GOETHE

Is it possible for a helping person to be accepted in this nearly
closed village system? And if so, is it then possible to change
life in the village enough to encourage people to trust each other
more, care for and about their physical ills, begin to hope for a
less anguished and violent existence? With many reservations,
we can state that with skill, tact, and above all, deeply felt concern, outsiders can enter these villages and alter parts of them
significantly.

The next six chapters describe our intervention with the total
population of nine buildings, including the manager and maintenance staff, and people external to the buildings who render
important services to it, such as the D.S.S., police, hospital staff
and administrators, and storekeepers.

Our projects were based on the premise that many individuals
in the SRO population might be physically and/or emotionally
unable or unwilling to withstand the stress and, for some, the
humiliation of seeking traditionally rendered services in institutional settings; hence a more effective way to reach them might
be to offer help to the total social group in the home setting.
We assumed that the multi-problem individual, despite psychological scars which have placed him outside family life, has the
capacity to create affective ties with others in his environment,
and that strengthened relationships resulting from group cohesion would reduce isolation, loneliness, despair and apathy. We

also assumed that self-destructive behavior of individuals could be modified, not by psychotherapy but by changes in the environment. We would create a more benign social milieu by heightening meaningful social contact and by providing opportunities and space for passive and active recreational activities and gratifications (8).

Through these changes we expected that pressure upon individuals to express extreme stress in deviant or violent ways would be reduced, and other channels for expression in the social situation would be provided.

The workers would view themselves as catalytic agents. They would focus on the positives, the evidence, however slender, of the tenants' wish for productive and satisfying social experience and for the avoidance of loneliness and pain. They would stress the strengths rather than the pathology. Their optimism, vitality, and faith in the healing potential of group experience as a vehicle for renewed growth would create for them and tenants alike a powerful self-fulfilling prophecy, where hope could be regenerated.

Tentative goals were: 1) to organize the tenants into a group or groups to share activities and/or problems; 2) to expand and strengthen mutually protective relationships; 3) to extend individuals' capacities to want help and to withstand the frustrations of seeking it; 4) wherever possible to bring about changes in institutional intake procedures to correspond to the special needs of this population.

Methodological Roots

Many streams of knowledge and experience have influenced our approach to the SRO as a self-help community. Among them are applied anthropology, with its combined goals of preserving the ethos of a particular people while helping to alter those patterns which endanger survival in a rapidly changing world. A second is milieu therapy (7) (21) in which the patient becomes part of the therapeutic team on behalf of his own and others' treatment. Its more specific extension in group work, practiced in the psychiatric hospital, applies group-work skills to a mentally ill population by working primarily to improve their ego strength in dealing with reality problems (23).

A third and most closely analogous model is the socialization of the street gang by the detached group worker (3). The New York City Youth Board pioneered in this field (18). The worker, alone and detached physically from his agency, offers only himself, his personality, integrity and skill. Problems of initial contact, of establishing rapport, of value conflicts, of structuring his role, and finally, of using his relationship with the gang to change socially destructive and self-destructive behavior, have many parallels to work in the SROs. The worker's task is the same: to influence the behavior of a partly formed group on the group's—not the worker's—home territory.

Finally, William Schwartz's (24) conceptualization of the social work function in the mediation model has sanctioned and enriched our work with the systems impinging on the lives of the tenants. Most of the project student-workers had been taught by him and were deeply influenced by his work. In his words:

> The general assignment for the social work profession is to mediate the process through which the individual and his society reach out for each other through a mutual need for self-fulfillment. This presupposes a relationship between the individual and his nurturing group which we would describe as "symbiotic" each needing the other for its own life and growth, and each reaching out to the other with all the strength it can command at a given moment. The social worker's field of intervention lies at the point where two forces meet: the individual's impetus toward health, growth, and belonging; and the organized efforts of society to integrate its parts into a productive and dynamic whole (p. 7).

The Projects

The earliest of the nine projects was begun in 1964, the last in 1967. I was the worker in the first project using the model of intervention here described. While a wide range of helping people, most of them nonprofessionals, has been engaged in some aspect of the work, there was in each project one head worker. Some projects had a succession of two or three workers. Of the total of thirteen, two were trained psychiatric social workers, six were social group work students who had a nine-month field placement with the St. Luke's Hospital Center, Division of Community Psychiatry, three were college students working with us for the summer, two were former SRO tenants who became employed paraprofessionals. All but four were supervised by me. The workers' functions in three buildings have been taken over successfully by D.S.S. workers, some of whom I also trained in this method.

All workers, whether staff of St. Luke's Hospital Center's Community Psychiatry Division or students placed there for field experience, spent about two days a week in their project buildings. They worked with groups and individuals within each building, with referral agencies, and with people living in the neighboring community, and recorded these experiences in detail. In addition, workers made themselves available to help in crisis situations. As the projects gained momentum and indigenous leaders became increasingly active, the workers' participation tended to be reduced. No special funding for salaries was needed since the work was part of the normal work load of the agency. The only cash expenditures were for food and emergency carfare, which amounted to $150 monthly for a typical building of about 100 tenants. This was partly donated by the hospital and partly by interested members of the community, who also contributed equipment such as TV sets, record players, records, books, and furniture, or lent a motion picture projector, films and screen. Some also volunteered time to assist in activities within the buildings, such as sewing classes, community sings, church services, and remedial reading.

Entry Phase

The work in the buildings can be divided into three overlapping phases: 1) entry; 2) program development and the process through which it occurred; and 3), termination, which, in two buildings, included relocation.

There were several patterns common to the entry phase of the projects. The opening encounters between workers and tenants, tenant leaders, and managers were painful, conflicted, yet exhilarating experiences. Over a period of time, usually no longer than eight weeks, the distance, caution and mistrust between them generally decreased at a rate which permitted comfort for each of them. Certain managers and tenants never established more than a formal relationship of pleasantries with the worker, and those few workers, an exception to the general trend, were never able to permit an intensity of involvement with tenants.

While the setting is the SRO, the initial entry process, its special problems and satisfactions, can be generalized to many situations of detached work in the community; that is, in situations where the helping person of any profession arrives uninvited and unheralded on the territory of the potential recipient of help, and must find ways of beginning a dialogue by offering his own personality, integrity and skill to convey the wish to help.

I have delineated in Chapter I our growing body of knowledge about the SRO dwellers' life-style; at the time the projects were begun, much was unknown and the expectations of the workers largely conformed to the cultural norm. The SRO evoked a stereotyped vision of a cluster of solitary individuals with few, if any, social skills, negligible family or other contacts, and with rootless, drifting ways of life producing indifference to personal ties and neighborhoods.

A fear of violence beset the workers, specifically the fear that the worker might be the victim of violence or of sexual attack. There was, of course, a rational concomitant to this fear. Many violent acts did occur in or near such buildings. They were the source of chronic police calls; neighbors expressed their fear and aversion by avoiding passing the front stoop, and tended to attribute every criminal act within a four- or five-block area to the tenants. Visiting nursing agencies formalized this fear by not allowing the nurses to enter such buildings. Thus the worker was faced with a fear to which the community and professionals alike responded; these fears had to be overcome sufficiently to permit even an initial approach to the building.

The worker's emotional journey into the lives of the tenants proceeded from distance to intimacy, from focus on the self to focus on the tenants, and from fear of interaction to pleasure in it. In anticipation of the moment of approaching the building, the manager and the first tenant, each worker grappled with anxieties about the client and fear about his own capacity to do the job. Each carried to some extent a stereotyped image of the SRO resident, with mixed feelings of pity, fear, and disgust. There was an awareness that these people had been given up as patients and clients by most service systems because of their "lack of motivation," irresponsibility, and noncomprehension of the needs of the system for promptness, patience, and "proper papers."

Entirely alone in a setting in which professional values, tradition, and customary role performances had no apparent ready application, the worker usually felt even methods and goals to be vague. Formidable questions about his role and the task confronted him. Could such isolated individuals relate sufficiently to create a viable group? How much work with individuals should be attempted, if any? Was the manager or the Department of Social Services worker a client? Should the primary target be the community groups who wanted the building closed? Was he to be a group worker, a community organizer, an educator, a generic mental health worker, a sociologist, a foster parent, a consultant? Then again, how should the worker define the population to be serviced? Within one SRO, the target could include all tenants, or a series of individuals on any one floor or along one corridor, or, alternately, those on welfare, or those employed, or all over sixty-five, or all alcoholics, or social clusters of those who drink together, or the ex-mental hospital patients, or the manager and his staff. Each worker responded in his unique way to the stress and ambiguity, and experienced a personal and professional identity crisis.

Opening Negotiations with Managers

The workers' first task was to obtain the permission of each manager to set up a recreation-rehabilitation program. No manager openly opposed the offer of help to his tenant group, but all showed caution, with a few showing anxiety when approached by the workers. The opening encounters ranged from covert resistance to open helpfulness. The following records a worker's opening experience:

Some of the tenants were sitting out on the stoop and ignored my presence. The manager appeared to be quite reluctant about having a worker and expressed his doubts and anxiety and thought a worker's presence might cause further problems. An active effort was made to assure him, and finally I reached him with "I'm not on the tenants' side, but here for you too." The manager finally began to show some interest. He reiterated the fact that there were no alcoholics, etc., in the building, and that whenever he found there was an alcoholic or prostitute, he made every effort to evict that person. His attitude, although understandable, was somewhat depressing because the tenants seemed only to be economic entities to him. I also felt that the prestige of a hospital connection made him accept the idea of a worker in the building, which he really did not relish, and whose purpose he did not understand.

In a dramatic meeting, one manager's deep bitterness, despair and frustration were expressed to a worker, who was moved to respond to him not as an enemy, but as a client:

. . . I said "Is there any way that I can help you in the building with some of the tenants, to make things a little easier? Perhaps I could intercede in some things or help out a problem that you can't handle or need assistance with." Mr. X. did not know what to say and then laughed. "You can't help me. I'm beyond help. I'm hopeless." There was another pause, and Mr. X. continued: "You would have to be here 24 hours a day because everything goes wrong when I'm not here." Someone came to the window, and he motioned for me to watch. One of the tenants was harassing him about money, and Mr. X. was quite brutal back to him. The tenant left, and he turned to me and said, "You ought to come here on check day and see what happens with all the welfare money." He talked for quite a long time about tenants not being able to handle their money, being lazy and how he couldn't understand how they threw away all the chances they had. I listened without saying anything. Finally Mr. X. said to me, "I'm glad that you got the picture so fast of how rotten this place is."

As I began leaving, I said that it was good talking to him. I understood things much more clearly. Mr. X. gladly exclaimed, "What good is it—it's given me a catharsis to talk everything out of me?" I laughed and said that that was not the purpose, but if that was what had happened, I guess it was all for the better. There was a silence, and I asked Mr. X. if he was all alone in trying to manage. Mr. X. answered that it is better to be without anyone and told me a story of a partner who had pushed him more than the tenants. Finally, he said, "My father sits in the office in the back and keeps pushing me and pushing me about why did I do this and why I did that. The tenants push me from the other side, but it's better that I'm alone in this, because all I need is another partner to really foul things up." There was another pause, and he said that he would be glad to help me. I said that I didn't know how things would work out, but I would promise that the program would not hinder him—I would like to work with him, not against him. Mr. X. laughed and said that was fair enough, and I told him I would be back in the building Thursday. We shook hands, and I left.

Opening Encounters with Tenants

In the opening contact with the tenants the workers struggle to move toward the client, yet simultaneously to master anxiety. The tenants are sensitive to the worker's dilemma and some are skilled in helping him. The mutual nature of the relationship seems clear as we see the process of testing and bargaining between them. The tenant leaders, in some instances, seem to elicit from the workers the qualities and behavior which they need, and communicate this verbally and nonverbally.

Overoptimism, denial, and intellectualization were used by workers to overcome unmanageable anxiety. Each of these attitudes enabled a delaying action which helped the workers master their fears and move closer to their clients.

In one project, the worker in her first two visits found herself profoundly impressed by the initial welcome the tenants extended to her. Her "noble savage" image of them was only later balanced by a perception of the amount of pathology, pain, hunger and fear visible in the building.

One student worker postponed going to the building, then arranged to be accompanied; when there, she spoke only to the landlord and left. It took several weeks of this kind of skirmish before she was able to notice the tenants in the lobby and began to be able to individualize them.

Others had more specific fears; one common one is fear of physical proximity or sexual assault.

It was my first visit to an SRO. I kept mouthing all the comforting phrases which I had heard at the office: "They're just people. The murders, face slashings are all exaggerated." I had never seen an addict in my life; would he know what I was thinking? I politely entered the room and extended my hand to everyone who came up to me. One man, large and disfigured, squeezed my hand hard; he would not let go. I guess my face showed a flash of panic and I tried to jerk my hand away. Another tenant, seeing my need, came over and whispered to me, "You just gently ease your hand away and talk to him." It worked.

What often appeared to be a sexual approach was bravado, a thinly disguised hunger for closeness and dependency, and recognized as such by the leaders and eventually by the workers.

The following is a first-day record where a sexual approach by a woman is deftly read by the male worker as defensive:

When I came downstairs, the same woman was still shouting at her girl friend. She came over to me and said, "Who the hell are you, mother-f – – – – –?" She was obviously drunk; she was a short, 46-year-old Negro, very disheveled and on crutches, but had a friendly smile, despite all her bluster. Each time I tried to explain who I was, she would interrupt with more profanity. I finally told her if she didn't shut the f – – – up, I couldn't tell her what I was there for. This vastly amused her and she asked me to help her up to her room, as it was difficult for her to walk. We had a talk on the way about why she wanted the girl next door thrown out of the building, how the building was full of nuts, and how nobody could f – – – with her. She then explained that she was worried about drinking too much and that when sober, she was nothing like this. She asked me for money for booze, and I told her no. After a great deal of quite good-natured arguing, she gave in, told me I was as stubborn as she was. She said that what she wanted now was for the two of us to screw, but I replied, "I'm sorry, baby, but however attractive I think you are, I've got to keep my screwing and social work separate." This brought on about a minute of very hard laughing by both of us. She then lay down, and I sat there quietly as she rolled out the story of her life, her graduation from a university, her career as a non-com in the Army, her marriage to an alcoholic husband whom she loved, witnessing his death, her mother's taking her son to raise, her numerous lesbian incidents, and the onset of drinking. When she finished her story, she shut her eyes, opened them again a few times to make sure I was staying, and finally passed out. After I was certain she was asleep, I pulled the cover over her, shut off the light, and went downstairs.

One worker plunged quickly into many contacts with tenants, denying her fears and uncertainties by viewing herself as an urban anthropologist, one step removed from the excitement and condescension of "slumming." Another made meticulous attempts to obtain statistical data; however, within weeks, a "datum" became a person and the initial crisis was over for her.

My own fear and uncertainty were reflected in vacillation about whether or not to take my purse on the first visit. I decided to take the purse, a gesture carefully rationalized as being respectful of the tenants and of myself. I later learned that it was widely and carefully noted by the tenants I met that day and helped to ease the initial mutual mistrust. Reviewing the incident, I now feel that the decision was partly counterphobic, an exaggerated personal assertion of optimism and trust that I did not wholeheartedly feel but which, had I known it, was justified.

In projects begun after the initial one, workers were increasingly well prepared to expect certain patterns: the manager's reciprocal relationship to the tenants, the probable existence of friendship groups, the presence of profound illness and deviance. He also could expect a difficult period of "culture shock" in his own life. But as workers approached their task, this knowledge was only peripherally useful. The initial contact for each was a unique adventure, a total engulfing experience in which intellectual concepts only gradually became usable knowledge, integrated emotionally into that person's experience.

As workers entered into the novel world of the SRO, they explored a new culture where the language, customs, and social order had to be learned. Some workers were not too disturbed by the absence of a ready-made role for themselves and could allow themselves to be taught. This entailed learning to use and feel comfortable with the tenants' style of communication, i.e., physical expressiveness. It also entailed at first giving and then receiving things. Cigarettes were often the initial means of symbolic sharing, lighting one another's cigarettes a ceremonial game. When workers were proffered one, it was a gift of an expensive commodity.

The tenants were also in a stressful learning situation. They had to evaluate an unexpected knocking on the door, to understand this invasion of their privacy, to make a decision whether to encourage or reject the situation and then allow further developments.

The following is the recollection of a dynamic matriarch of her initial meeting with the worker:

I expected her to be a sweet, fake, older lady with lots of money, and when I heard she was downstairs, I told the bunch in my room . . . "God damn it, don't breathe, don't show no bottles. I want no shit out of you." Then I went downstairs and there she was, plain and businesslike, and I was very polite; but I thought, what is that bitch doing here? It was queer, and I was scared. I asked her to come upstairs, and they were all on their best behavior. But the one thing that was so warm about her was she carried her handbag and put it down and left it on my bed and went down the hallway to meet some more tenants; I said to myself, "This woman is crazy, but I like her, but I don't really know, is she for real or playing the part of a good confidence woman." I couldn't have a drink, since I was supposed to be a leader, and with our reputation, that's all we needed.

Opening Encounters with Groups

By the time the worker has stimulated enough interest for a first group meeting, small or large, much of the fear and anxiety is behind him. The crucial questions become those of strategy and skill: Who are the dominant leaders of subgroups? Is there enough basis for cooperation between them? What is to be the content of group interaction? What are their problems or sources of pleasures? There are many overlapping subgroups in the SROs with varying degrees of influence. If the worker were to relate to any one subgroup exclusively, it might jeopardize impact upon other subgroups; the worker could not afford to become an ally of any one segment without complex and unpredictable consequences to the whole. In one building, the worker became very comfortably accepted by one subgroup, only to find that she had unwittingly become identified with this single segment and could include others only with some difficulty.

A planning meeting, at which two of the four tenants present were, unbeknownst to the worker, dominant social leaders in the building, and the first tenants' meeting which followed were described:

My first meeting was with three nonresident, political organizers and four tenants in a tiny, dark room. It contained a bed, a dresser with some handles missing, two straight chairs and one window opening on a narrow court. The neatness and cleanliness of the room contrasted ironically with the decaying linoleum, torn plastic curtains, peeling paint, roaches, and dilapidated furniture, and no storage space. There was a small radio, no clock, no TV and no books.

At first I was invited to sit on the bed. The organizers pressed their request for group therapy for tenants discharged from mental hospitals. The four tenants were silent. Puzzled, I kept asking how many this involved and who had requested the service. It then became clear that the organizers thought that this would give the hotel a better image. It might also serve to control violent behavior conspicuous in the community, in order to strengthen their pending court case banning the reconversion of the building by the owner for other uses. The ex-mental patients had not been asked. Pointing this out, I then turned to the tenants present, who were suspicious and clearly frightened, caught between the organizers and myself in a serious ideological difference: they using the tenants for predetermined goals of their own to which they were deeply committed and feeling they were acting on behalf of these and all tenants, and I, unable to accept this step without prior total involvement and decision-making on the part of the tenants themselves. To my query, "What would you think might be helpful?" one man said, "If we really told you, you would say, ever so politely, 'I'm sorry, we don't offer that.' Social workers are all alike." I said he was right in that at this moment, I didn't have a thing to offer. They were taken aback by this—the mood changed and they began to describe the people who are dying, who won't go to the hospital, the hospitals which turn their people away, the welfare investigators who are always thinking that you can work when, if they'd take a look, they'd see you can't. Citing an example, one perky lady with charm and a sharp tongue, said that a card for a job interview had come for a friend of hers who was a 68-year-old addict with a heart condition. She also spoke of the loneliness of some people. I said I thought that these things we could work on together—getting better medical care, getting better cooperation from welfare and finding ways of connecting people up to each other in the building—provided the tenants really wanted these things and would work on them.

By this time, the organizers were silent. I said that we could only find out what tenants would want by asking. In the remaining time, we decided to have a building-wide meeting, and struggled with different ideas as to how to get the most attendance—food, room-by-room word-of-mouth (door knocking) and signs. I arranged to ask the manager for use of an empty room. We broke up on an excited note. I also suggested to the organizers that they bring up the group therapy and court case there to see what kind of interest they could stimulate.

The first large tenants' meeting was held in an empty large room given by the manager. About fifty tenants attended, as well as a half dozen of the outside organizing group. The four tenants in the earlier meeting had obviously worked hard to get people to come and were still fetching shy or reluctant ones well after the meeting started—one hour later than planned. As the meeting began the worker was obviously being challenged and tested by both groups, and it was difficult to switch the focus from interrogation by the organizers to a tenant-focused meeting. I tried to encourage discussion of the possibilities of a program of the tenants' own devising and participation. The tenants then timidly began to come forward with many suggestions: a recreation program, a gym class for men, a separate reading and knitting corner for women, television, church services, a billiard table, medical service in the building, psychiatric referrals, a methadon clinic in the building and a workshop. Unrealistic suggestions were challenged by other tenants, while some were accepted and discussed further. There was no response to the worker's query about group therapy. Several organizers left halfway through the meeting.

The first impression of the characteristics of this tenant group was later corroborated by more extensive findings. The group was largely Negro with a small scattering of Puerto Rican men and white women. Many seemed over forty, malnourished, and wearing dilapidated clothing. About a third of the tenants showed signs of intoxication and two were "nodding" as a drug reaction during the meeting. This fact did not in any way deter the meeting from continuing and many contributions were made by people who seemed quite drunk; the group as a whole showed tolerance for this behavior. Two people were rambling and incoherent; one was ridiculed into silence and the other quietly maneuvered out of the room. This was the first indication of both protectiveness and restraint imposed by the group on individuals.

This tenant meeting was crucial in setting the stage for succeeding events. The differentiation of the tenants themselves—as well as their view of their needs—from the political organizers and their concept of the needs was made very clear. The tenants' participation in planning was begun. Natural leaders and the worker began to form an alliance which was central to the development of a program.

Any clear verbal statement between worker and tenants of what each may expect of the other and what work they are to do together has scarcely begun in the foregoing illustrations. However, the negotiation in each case has begun. The social worker, in these encounters, may not yet be the helper. He is being tested and judged to determine his capacity to fit into a different world of which he soon may be a part.

During entry the respective roles to be taken by workers and tenants, and the rules governing their relationship, are established. The quality of their honesty and directness with one another in this phase, and their level of liking and respect for each other determine the intimacy, vitality and intensity of their encounters in successive phases of program development.

But, as can be seen in the foregoing, for the worker the process of developing clarity of purpose, ease and satisfaction was to be long and hard and matched by tenants' growth toward clarity of purpose, ease and satisfaction in their bargaining with the worker and in their participation in the program. False starts, over- and underestimates, playing the game of working together without conviction and investment, an appearance of trust before true trust developed, were characteristic of the early phase on both sides of the partnership. The beginning of the second, or work, phase was signaled by a bargain between tenants and worker to work toward common goals firmly based on trust.

3

Programs: From Recreation
to Problem Solving

Everybody here has a hangup; mine is different from yours—
no better, no worse; we've got this room—let's not get hung up
fighting about who's better, winos or junkies. We'll lose the whole
program that way.

—SRO TENANT

The work phase of the projects began with the agreement between the worker and a group within a building to work together
toward a definite goal. A sense of purposefulness and specificity
characterized their interaction. They agreed to solve a problem,
meet a need, perform an action together. Over a period of time
the content of their action changed repeatedly as the "contract"
between them was renegotiated. As problems were solved and
needs were met, new and more ambitious goals were agreed
upon and programs became complex and sometimes sophisticated.

Initial activities varied from building to building. In some
cases, the people with whom the worker first negotiated were
members of a single small subgroup; in others, they were the
dominant members from a number of different subgroups. The
activity undertaken then derived from the needs and interests of
those tenants who became the decision-makers. Most activities
were strongly housebound and oriented in the direction of building an ingroup. In several buildings enough tenants were so ill,
frightened or withdrawn that activities outside their own rooms
was difficult; for a long time these tenants were unable to con-
template any activities outside their buildings.

The programs achieved richness and variety because the tenants' activities were grounded in an already existing system of expectations of one another based on *mutual aid*. Workers nurtured, enriched and developed this system in their interventions to the point where not only one person was nurturing one or several others, but large groups of people were symbolically feeding and caring for one another. They shared the complexities of managing money, shopping, cooking and serving food to the shy, the sick and the bedridden. In like manner, the simple act of one person ministering to a sick neighbor flowered into taking on nursing roles for the whole building. These skills were given further impetus by the workers who increased the tenants' knowledge of outside resources and the negotiation of channels of communication. The already dominant tenant leaders were unquestionably the chief agents in these changes; they were the carriers of hope. Often they became the elected officers of tenants' associations, took responsibility and were closely identified with the worker.

They taught the workers to understand the inner life of the building. Through them the worker came to know the tenants and understand their most pressing life needs which were chronically unmet. Food, alcohol, money, cigarettes, a "fix," physical care and protection, or relationships which helped provide them, were highly valued and especially meaningful. Those innovations in the projects which dovetailed with these needs were quite successfully utilized; those which had no relevance were simply ignored.

Workers participated in the evolving group activities and were explicitly maternal in behavior, touching, feeding and establishing contact with individuals. At first they were available at all times and were most often used to mediate personal and group crises. Weekly tenants' meetings, planning meetings with indigenous leaders, and individual meetings with key people, including the manager, were held on a regular basis to give structure and continuity to the programs.

The beginning work tended to be a concrete service either for or with the tenants. For example, in one building a worker concentrated specifically on sick and dying tenants in cooperation with a tenant leader; in another, with a group of tenants, a worker requested use of an empty room; in a third, a worker contacted and set up a meeting between tenants and a Department of Social Services worker with whom communication had been difficult for the tenants.

A worker usually carried on simultaneously a number of individual contacts or met individual emergencies as they arose. In SROs, medical and financial crises and accidents are recurrent. The worker's handling of them was often a passport into the tenant system, and the tenants noted the worker's skill and knowledge about resources, and his prompt intervention.

When I got to the building Mary said that Mamie was in her room and that I should come up there right away. Mamie was sitting with a bloody cloth over her mouth. I asked what had happened and she said that someone had pushed her down the stairs. I asked her who did it and she said that Phil had done it. Mary took me into the kitchen and told me about the problems that Mamie and Phil had been having because he had been going out with someone else in the building.

I said that I thought that right now we should think about how we could help Mamie with the cut on her lip. I asked Mary what she thought should be done and she said that she thought that she should go to a doctor as soon as possible. I mentioned that medical group around the corner and asked her if she would take Mamie. She said that she was sick but that she would take her. I then said that I would call them first to see if they would take her so that they would not make an unnecessary trip.

This incident rapidly became gossip throughout the building.

Program Content

As the buildings and people varied, so did the shape and kind of program. Often the format at the beginning of programs centered on lounge-recreation activities and only later would problem-solving activities emerge. Setting up a recreation lounge presented a great many organizational challenges. The worker, and sometimes some tenant leaders, initially negotiated with the managers to get a room for such lounge activity. An essential step was to assure the manager that destructive or illegal behavior would not take place in this room; then to work out ways of maintaining, cleaning, and staffing it so that it was a source of pride and pleasure to the users. For many months, fighting, arguing and learning to share responsibilities were to be the chief activities of the tenants.

The lounge as an arena for developing cohesion and resolving conflicts had several advantages. It provided a place for passive entertainment for a large number of people without requiring prior social relationships. Daily responsibilities could be fragmented sufficiently to elicit wider participation in the sharing of tasks: one person was found to be willing to sweep occasionally, another to mend a table, a third to make a sign. The value of the lounge to the tenants was immediately palpable, especially when concrete services were introduced early, such as food, punch, a movie, group singing, cards or dancing.

The recreation room, as might be expected, usually became the stage for fierce territorial struggles between various subgroups. This record of a second meeting of an infant tenants' association shows tenants already setting limits and goals for themselves without active intervention by the worker.

The second large meeting of the tenants was followed by a party to celebrate opening of the recreation room. More than half the tenants of the building attended due to active door-knocking and careful preparation by leaders. One man was elected chairman of the recreation room and four men volunteered to give time to supervise it. Meanwhile, donations of a TV set, furniture, games, and a record player were made by interested community individuals, who continued throughout the program to contribute clothing, fabrics, food, and small amounts of money. The room had been freshly painted and some of the equipment was already in evidence. The tenants were excited and pleased.

During the meeting consensus was reached on a number of practical questions. Each of the decisions was painfully arrived at with much shouting, interrruption, and disagreement. The elected chairman, having had no experience in discussion leadership, was tentative in restoring order. Nevertheless, decisions were made: No drinking or nodding would be allowed in the room. No individual could bring his own food to eat there, as this was difficult for those who had none. Friends of tenants could use the recreation room only by prior arrangement with the chairman. There would be weekly tenants' meetings to discuss problems as they came up and to expand the program into other areas.

Within the lounge format, more complex activities began to take place. Among the most important and widespread was the decision of tenant groups to create regularly scheduled building-ing-wide dinners, especially at holiday times—Thanksgiving, Christmas, and Easter. Since these are culturally signaled times of reunion, people without families are especially vulnerable to depression. In SROs heavy drinking and conspicuous disturbances usually occur during these holidays. To counteract this, tenants and workers made the planning and sharing of meals an activity of central importance. How to decide on the menu, who was to buy the food, how this money was to be negotiated, who was to cook, how it was to be set up, who was to serve it, who was to clean up, were all matters of an intensely experienced group process. In SRO groups there are usually a number of people who have had experience in the restaurant or catering business, so skills in the preparation of food were almost always available. We often tried to provide much more food than the entire building could eat because we had observed that greediness was marked; a great deal of overeating or hiding of food in clothing had been noted. We hoped, therefore, to provide a symbolic and actual sense of abundance by enabling people to have as many portions as they wished, and then to take some with them. Those who could not come to the dinners were served in their rooms if they wanted to be. Soon this same principle of generous feeding was adopted by the tenants who extended it to feeding unpopular tenants as well as sick ones. In two buildings, lists of those who did not get dinner were made up and earnest attempts were made to see that no one was left out.

As programs evolved, they filled every day with minor excitement, involving people as participants rather than as spectators. A case in point was the recreation room: "Is it open yet?" "What time does it open?" "Who will be there?" "Let's go down and play cards." "The TV was supposed to be fixed and brought back Tuesday. Is this Tuesday?" "The meeting is at five; I have to iron my shirt today to get ready." "My clinic appointment is tomorrow; I'll wash my hair today." "The Thanksgiving dinner is next week; maybe I can buy a belt out of my next check so my pants don't sag."

Into the sluggish, flat landscape, the workers brought events, dates, and new subtle demands for conformity with outside expectations. Attention was paid to the time of a meeting or dinner, the date of a forthcoming appointment and seasonal celebrations.

A Christmas party is described by a student worker who had been working in the building for two months:

Harriet served sandwiches and stuff on plates to most of the people who came in. In the first part, I mostly just introduced people who did not know each other, and helped people take plates up to the bedridden or sick ones. The main topic of conversation was Joyce's new baby, who had just come that day, and not everyone knew the sex and size of the little baby. . . .

Later on, talking to the latecomers who were eating, Harriet came in the room, singing "Auld Lang Syne." Almost at once we all joined in, and it sounded beautiful. We went into Christmas carols. We had trouble with the pitch on one, and Big Jim said something about a piano. Harriet said that she used to play a swell saxophone, but because of her heart, she could not. It took too much wind. Everyone said that was a shame, couldn't she play anything? And she said nothing. I said I thought she played a harmonica. Charley jumped up and asked if I had one with me. I said no, and Harriet said maybe she could get her bells, and Charley said that he had a harmonica; and everyone whooped because it was so great an idea, even in anticipation. They came back, and we sang more carols, even Big Jim. Jimmy would get up and make loud unmelodic noises, and he had a skirmish with Harriet over his missing bottle but several people shut him up. I patted him on the shoulder once when he was trying to be quiet. When I took my hand away he told me to put it back, which I did, and he started to sing a great bass.

It was beautiful in sound, and in a pause someone said so. I said that it seemed like everyone was a little surprised at how great we did sound, and Big Jim said well, everyone knows the words; Manny complimented Harriet and Charley on the instruments, which did help.

Then singing "O Little Town of Bethlehem," there were tears in our eyes, when we came to "Yet in the dark street shineth the everlasting light," and after a silence after the song, I said, "and Joyce had her baby . . ." because that was what I was thinking about in connection with the song, and said, "That is our little baby," and Jimmy said it was like the baby Jesus. Everyone was silent for a little while, thinking about that, and Harriet said as I opened my mouth to say the same thing . . . "I have an idea . . ." Immediately everyone knew what we were going to say, and we started to practice what we were going to sing when we went up to carol for the baby. Howard came in the midst of it to eat, and was encouraged to come along, though he insisted he could not sing. Jimmy made a noise and Betty and Manny told him they would fix him if he didn't keep himself straight.

When we went to the elevator, it was with admonishments of silence till we knocked on the door, Howard with his plate of food, Jimmy staggering between Charley and me, and general hilarity and seriousness, if such a combination is possible. In the elevator I said it was really like a pilgrimage and Jimmy said yeah, we have to sing for the baby. Charley nodded, and Harriet told him to shut up, we were almost there.

After some shuffling outside the door, we knocked and Joyce came to the door, holding the baby. Everyone took a breath in surprise at the perfection of the timing, and we sang. Joyce was speechless and beautiful, just glowing; and the baby dug the singing. She did not even cry when Jimmy leaned over and kissed her or when the singing got loud and confused.

After we sang the two songs we planned, everyone chorused "Merry Christmas," and scampered back to the elevator, which was even there waiting for us! Back downstairs, everyone collapsed and congratulated one another, and went over it all. Harriet said she knew Joyce was touched because she couldn't even say anything. Then there were all the discussions of how superior the baby is, and what a groovy chick (as Jimmy put it) she is to dig our singing. I said that she seemed to be a little bit of everyone's baby. Harriet and Jimmy said emphatically that she was, to be sure.

A second development, common somewhat later in the program, was creating other forms of activities in the lounges
Watching television, which again involved the guaranteeing of
the safety of the TV from theft, learning to police its use in such
a way that it would not be broken, deciding on which programs
to watch when there was a difference of opinion—all were major
issues, discussed and argued out for weeks on end. In two buildings, in spite of the fact that a television set was available to the
tenants, they voted not to use it for several months because they
did not feel safe enough among themselves to trust one another
with its care.

Card games in some buildings were perennial, magazines and
books became available in libraries which developed in two
buildings. Movies were shown in several buildings; there were
religious services in another, and in one building in which there
was considerable musical and dramatic talent, a talent show developed spontaneously.

Posted announcements in a single building illustrate the development of typical program content in a nine-month period.

(1)

TENANTS OF 404!
ON JULY 14
A LOUNGE
IN THE BASEMENT
WILL BE OPEN TO
TENANTS ONLY
OPEN 5 – 7 PM
REFRESHMENTS WILL BE SERVED

(2)

RECREATION ROOM RULES

1. There will be no drinking in the recreation room.
2. There will be no gambling in the recreation room.
3. Men will kindly remove their hats when entering the room
4. Any person who is loud, or who disturbs others will be
   politely asked to leave. If he does not do so, the management of the hotel will be asked to evict him from the room
5. No one is to help himself to food. Ask the hostess and she
   will be glad to serve you.

All these rules have been decided by the steering committee. If you have any questions, suggestions, or complaints, please talk with a member of the committee.

K.C	W.J.	A.R.	E.T.
W.C.	C.M.	R.S.	N.W.
R.D.	W.M.	M.T.	

(3)

November 12

Dear Tenants:

There will be a Tenants Association Dinner on Monday night, November 15th, at 5:30 P.M. The menu will be:

FRIED CHICKEN
MACARONI AND CHEESE
CABBAGE
PUNCH

Fred has again offered to be our cook—that guarantees it will be a great dinner.

Very truly yours,
Mary P.
Chairman

(4)

TO TENANTS OF 404

There will be an Important meeting
on Jan. 13th at 5:00 P.M. to decide
about ways to get to the Hospital.

(5)

SPRING FASHION SHOW
featuring
TENANTS OF 404
as models
will be held
in the
Recreation Room
on the evening of
THURSDAY, MAY 11 at 7:30 P.M.
ADMISSION FREE
ALL   ARE   WELCOME

(6)

COME TO
A
GIANT GOODBYE
PARTY
FOR
KATHY *

May 25th   —   Eats for all

Some tenants developed a strong desire to break out of the
confines of the building. Trips to the beach, downtown, boat
rides, and movies became a new arena for confidence and
pleasure. The constant theme of these moves out of the building
was the effort to break through the defensive barriers which
many tenants had built against the outside world because of
feeling ugly, conspicuous, poorly dressed and unacceptable.
Although enthusiastic plans were frequently drawn up for trips
and excursions, these sometimes came to nothing as the people
involved could not face those first steps outside the building. In
some instances, this was in fact for want of proper clothing. In
other instances, the first move outside the building as a group
had to be an extremely limited local one. Fear of new experiences, anxiety about being able to behave appropriately, as well
as concern that other tenants might shame the group, were
lively and painful considerations in trip planning. Last-minute
dropouts were common. But most of those who went were exhil-
arated and exhausted by the experience. Always, one or two got
drunk. On a trip to the beach, one woman became psychotic and
walked heedlessly into deep water. For these reasons, trips had
to be carefully planned and heavily supervised.

Some workers tried to focus in the early weeks on the overwhelming problems of poverty, housing, illness, alcoholism or
addiction, believing that these were the most obvious areas in
which to find common ground for work. The invariable response
of tenants in the group situation was uneasy silence, embarrassment or clowning. The tenants could separate the possible from

* The student worker whose field placement was over.

the impossible with far greater accuracy than the young middle-class workers.

More immediate pleasure producing group experience—the sharing of food, a party, watching ball games on a donated TV: these were the necessary precursors to more emotionally charged and risk-laden activities of the second phase.

These activities, too, were concrete and limited in scope and time: a small loan fund, group support of increased use of health facilities, negotiation with managers for improved services or on behalf of a tenant facing eviction. In only two buildings were groups of tenants able to make formal connection with outside block associations and welfare rights groups.

As tenants' groups matured, they were able to use their experiences to solve complex problems and plan for themselves.

Loan Fund

The tenants, especially those who were welfare recipients, were chronically short of funds before check day. Loan sharks (and sometimes managers) would fill this vacuum by extending credit on a two-to-one, or even a three-to-one basis. A form of loan fund was begun, based on credit union principles and controlled by the tenants. Repayments into the fund were on a one-to-one basis. Tenants could only borrow up to $2.00 and could not borrow again until the previous loan was repaid. The initial deposit of $25 or more to begin the fund came from the program money given by the hospital and used by the tenants' association in whatever way the participating tenants collectively wished. A building with $100 monthly to spend could, in any one month, put aside money for the fund or replenish it. The opening discussions about a credit union which was to flourish in this building were recorded as follows:

The lack of money on the part of tenants came up again. People were not at all hesitant to discuss it. Henry said it wasn't poor planning, there just wasn't enough to plan with, if you were on welfare. I said I knew it was damn hard to stretch it for two weeks, but also wondered why there seemed to be more complaints now than I usually heard. People shrugged, and I asked if there were more expenses because of Christmas.

They seemed to feel it was just the general condition. I asked what they usually did when they were short of money. A few said they borrowed, some said they did nothing, and I said I'd heard they had to pay two-for-one when they borrowed. Some were angry in saying they sure did. I asked who they borrowed from, a tenant or someone outside the building and people were silent; someone said they wouldn't tell me. I assured them that I only asked for my own information and they certainly didn't have to tell me. They relaxed, and I said, "Well, I wondered if there was something we could do through our program to help remedy this situation"; we'd mentioned a credit union before the meeting got underway. Several people felt this was a good idea. Henry said we should have one. Dick said it should be at the desk, right along with the carfare, but the manager vetoed this, saying he wouldn't be responsible for it and also felt people should have to pay back the next check day, so they'd have less money for the next two weeks. I asked, "Should there be a limit then?" and people agreed. Arthur suggested $5, and Paul said $3. I pointed out what would be left the next check day, if they had to pay back either $3 or $5, and people felt $3 would be closer to what they could handle. Henry said there should also be a limit on how often you could do it, so you didn't get to living ahead of your money always, and I agreed the reason for having a credit union was to get people out of trouble, not into more trouble. The group laughed and agreed.

The programs tended to stimulate movement of outsiders into the building: volunteers who taught sewing, students who came to sing folk songs, visiting dignitaries who became interested, photographers and newsmen, neighbors with clothing, food, or just plain curiosity. The D.S.S. worker now became a familiar figure. All these added an inflow of interest and friendliness. Most tenants became positively self-aware and proud of their accomplishments. A few felt intruded upon.

As people became more aware of the less visible members of the building population, their absence would be noticed and their illnesses and depressions cared for more actively. People began to care for each other much more extensively and to protect one another on an ongoing and reliable basis. This concern in several buildings formalized itself in Clinic Committees. Here a small group of tenants took formal responsibility for reminding people about appointments, helping them dress, negotiating for clinic cards, waiting with them in the emergency room of the hospital. They also became the "family" for a person needing to be hospitalized; they would visit him there, bring clothes and cigarettes, get signatures on welfare checks in order to pay the room rent, and bring him home again upon discharge. They also became able to help one another through crises, such as death, relocation and fear of hospitalization.

In this record, the worker helped the tenants convert their fear of death and anger at medical neglect into action.

When I entered the building, I heard Hank had died about 15 minutes earlier. I went to his floor and found five or six people outside his room, and others hanging around the hall. Sugar was there and crying very hard. Flick pushed me through saying I should look at him. The manager was trying to get people to leave so the police could finish their work.

Sugar said, "Hank is dead." I said I'd heard and that I was very sorry, I knew he was a close friend and that she felt terrible. We went to her room with Mug, Vincent and Flick. Sugar tried to tell the story of how he died, but Flick was being quite flip, saying it would happen to all of us and Hank had lived a good life. I said while this was true, it really didn't make you feel a lot better when you were upset. Flick said he was trying not to think about it; he couldn't believe it and it probably wouldn't hit him for a couple of weeks. Sugar said Hank had slept with Flick the night before, and now he was dead. She and Vincent and Mug were on the second floor drinking gin and when they got back to Sugar's room, they found Hank panting outside her door. He had apparently crawled up to her room from the 5th floor looking for help. Sugar had them take him down to his room and called an ambulance, but Hank died before it could come. They could hardly understand it, because he had been eating properly recently and had gotten pills from the hospital just a few days earlier. Mug said, "Just a couple of pills, what they gonna do for you?" Sugar said what did he expect, Hank was taking those pills, and more too. Flick said, "No, Hank was following instructions." They repeated the events that preceded Hank's death, and Flick said he should have seen something coming when Hank refused a drink the night before. Sugar seemed to feel very badly that they had been able to do nothing, saying over and over that they'd only been downstairs a short while and didn't know Hank needed them. I said this is often what we think about when someone dies, what we could have done to avoid it. They repeated that if only the ambulance had come, if only they'd realized last night he was sick, or been home. I said I hoped they realized that while they were very concerned with this, they didn't know that Hank was sick.

Flick and Vincent went to their rooms, and Sugar confided that Hank had lost bowel and urinary control just before he died and was upset at seeing the indignity of his death. I couldn't think of anything to say. I was moved more by Sugar's depth of feeling than by Hank's death and found myself weepy also.

Mug said, "The damn ambulance never came." I said, "Never came at all—you mean it wasn't just too late, it never came?" He was furious and rightly so. I said I'd been thinking about medical help a lot lately and was beginning to think we could do something through our program to get everyone better help. I wondered what they would think of working on this. Sugar nodded. I said I knew in other SROs they had done this, formed a committee to get to know clinic staff and arranged for people to go together to make the waiting easier and get better service. I asked if Sugar would be interested in this. She smiled, obviously pleased, and nodded and said yes in her shy way. I hugged her and said, "You know, we've got the whole world to conquer." Sugar said she would talk about it at the Friday meeting.

Before I left, I said it was good to just be with each other while they were so unhappy. Mug said he was going to take care of Sugar.

As a wider network of friendly contacts developed in the recreation room, increasingly more territory within the building was friendly and visitable. In two buildings the tenants association leaders extended themselves into the neighborhood block association and met with middle-class tenants, though this was initially a painful and frightening experience for them. Leaders in no other buildings were able to do this, though a few became active in the local Welfare Recipients League.

To conclude, programs had a patterned development which progressed from tentative first meetings through the establishment of a lounge program, to more complex committee-centered rehabilitative or community-oriented activities.

4

The Process of
Resolving Differences

> No one can cure another if he has not a genuine desire to help
> him; and no one can have the desire to help unless he loves, in
> the deepest sense of the word. . . .
>
> —S. NACHT

Tenants, worker and manager gradually accommodated their
goals and methods of relating to one another until they became
mutually compatible and acceptable, but the process of achiev-
ing an understanding of one another's needs and purposes was
difficult. All the participants had to settle important differences
and overcome obstacles to clear communication with each other.
Some points of friction developed between tenant leaders and
workers because of mutual mistrust and competitiveness, between workers and tenants about program, and between subgroups in the building who wanted territorial rights to the lounge.
Other differences were in relation to specific class-determined
value conflicts and expectations.

Workers and Leaders

The resolution of competitive conflict between workers and
the dominant matriarchs found in nearly every project building
was crucial to program development. Four of these women can
be described in some detail because they worked in parallel with
the workers in their buildings and became intimate with them.

These four had in common two characteristics: 1) They had
a large and stable following in a given building; and 2) they

functioned within the power that was bestowed upon them to support, nurture, heal and sometimes infantilize those in their care, in effect being a "good mother" to a highly dependent group of physically and emotionally ill people. In the microcosm of the SRO these four leaders had a high level of energy, the capacity to negotiate with the world outside and to remain active and resourceful in the face of poverty in comparison to their followers. The chronic crisis milieu of the SRO tends to perpetuate a pattern of leadership in which much authority is invested in one person, with stringently limited dispersion of independent decision-making and differential roles.

Despite their own emotional fragility, these leaders were central figures who stimulated and maintained the nucleus of social organization which evolved to cope with the extreme deprivation and loneliness of the tenants. They tried to organize and distribute the sparse material resources available, such as food, cigarettes, clothing, money, wine, and medication (including aspirin, antibiotics, and traquilizers). They also tried to organize an effective mutual aid system; to prevent decompensation or violence, where possible; to mediate for their followers for needed services at the hospital, the welfare center or the police station, and even to handle medical and psychiatric crises.

All four leaders were Negroes between the ages of forty and fifty-five. All were on welfare and had experienced lifelong family disorganization and poverty. Three of the four finished high school, an educational level five grades above the mean grade of the SRO population. All four were chronic alcoholics with severe medical problems: heart disease, high blood pressure, obesity, cirrhosis of the liver, pelvic inflammatory disease. Three of the four had been in jail at some time in their lives for assault, petty larceny, or drug pushing.

A sociometric analysis of interaction in one of the buildings with 104 tenants shows that one of the four leaders was chosen by a total of 40 tenants as a desired partner with whom to share activities; the leader herself chose seven tenants. Thus, more than one-third of the tenants in this building wished to have a fantasied or real relationship with her. We do not have sociograms for the other three leaders, but the strong impression is that a similar situation existed in their respective buildings.

This degree of affection and dependence seemed to be stimulated by the leaders' capacity to fulfill to some extent several basic needs: 1) direct oral gratification; 2) setting limits; and 3) assurance of support for the individual. The following are examples of each type of activity on the part of the four women.

Direct Oral Gratification

Mrs. Smith picks up, and has others pick up, cigarette butts which she keeps in an open jar in her room; anyone out of cigarettes can help himself.

Mrs. Crawford regularly collects large quantities of surplus foods from Welfare and keeps cooked dishes warm and ready to feed tenants who have run through their welfare checks on wine or drugs, or who have been rolled. Mrs. Crawford also recognizes the symptoms of D.T.'s and keeps wine hidden for such an emergency.

Setting Limits

Mrs. Johnson shames people who fight dangerously or argue abusively by calling the group's attention to their behavior. In extreme cases she will call on a strong ex-boxer to halt the fight. She does not intercede with those in the building whom she does not know well.

Seven tenants regularly turn over their welfare checks to Mrs. Crawford, who then doles out a dollar or so a day until the next check is received. Those using this system give the following reasons: They are less frequently robbed, they do not drink it all away, and they are not hungry on the last days before check day. Mrs. Crawford does not gain materially from her banking services.

Mrs. Smith has an extensive knowledge as well as a miscellaneous supply of psychiatric drugs. She encourages those who have come from state hospitals to stay on their prescribed drug regimen, and, on occasion, gives an acutely disturbed tenant some form of tranquilizer.

Assurance of Support

Mrs. Burns visits many of the bedridden tenants in her building, feeding them and nursing them. She takes care of the burial arrangements if, as is usually the case, no family appears. When a senile tenant whom she had looked after for years died, she took up a collection from other tenants to prevent burial in Potter's Field.

Mrs. Smith is aware of the arrival of new tenants and finds ways to help some of them into the social life of the building. By this route, they become grateful to her and subsequently loyal.

The intrusion of the worker into these leaders' lives and turf was accompanied in all instances by some tension and subtle conflict between them. This was usually worked out in the opening phase, and as a close relationship was established, each learned from the other. The leaders were invariably sensitive to the worker's anxieties and doubts and made it possible to delineate a helpful role. In response to a "You must be upset" cliché, a leader told one worker angrily, "Don't go by the social workers' book with us!" Her sensitivity to emotional dishonesty and mechanical interventions encouraged the worker to develop a style of helping that could be trusted by the tenant group. Other workers had analogous experiences. This style of interaction as learned from the leaders included touching, hugging, physical nearness, mutual sharing of cigarettes, the giving and accepting of food, and visible, direct, immediately emotional responsiveness. Increasingly attention, delight, annoyance, boredom, anxiety, admiration and affection were openly expressed between worker and tenants as they became able to share this style of relating to one another.

One worker made note of the evolution of her sense of comfort and intimacy with tenants during a period of nine months. Not only does physical distance decrease, but mutual exchange, giving *and* receiving, becomes possible. Her list follows:

First day:	Taking my purse; dressing nicely to go there.
	Being able to stay alone.
	Having them show me around.
	Offering them a cigarette.
Second day:	Going to C.'s room alone (a matriarch in the building).
	Staying for dinner.
Third day:	S. saying, "Don't touch the lady!" I flinching, then relaxing.

Second week:	Dancing with them at the first party.
	Accepting cigarettes from them.
	Shaking hands when we meet each other.
Second month:	Giving money for spending.
	Going off and leaving my purse with people I knew.
Third month:	Borrowing pots and pans for them.
	Bringing my own butter.
	Drinking spiked punch.
Thereafter:	Hugging some of them.
	Taking C. to a middle-class building across the street to introduce her.
	Lending my records and record player.
	Splitting a beer.
	Sitting on their beds.
	Eating foods that were new for me.
	Using their bathrooms.
	Washing a dying incontinent tenant.

Tenant leaders usually sensed the workers' ambivalence, and regulated the rate at which they revealed themselves in areas posing severe conflict for the worker, responding sensitively to nuances indicating acceptance or nonacceptance.

The bond between one tenant leader and her worker is reflected in this vignette which demonstrates her idealization and predominantly positive identification. The tenant reported:

Gradually Ann [the worker] and I had begun to trust each other and we used to talk to each other about my problems and if Rickey and I were fighting, she would come and talk to us, stating you can't lead the people if you are going to carry on yourselves. She never took sides. Then in her own cunning way she asked me would I like to go to a psychiatrist—if she could arrange it. I told her yes, but I wanted someone that didn't work by the book and look down on you like a tramp and I got a doctor, one that let you relax. Ann had talked to welfare and the Hospital about it and fixed it up. Every tenant loves and respects her. The tenants wouldn't do anything to hurt her. She puts herself in your place and she will move mountains if she can.

Through identification and learning processes, the leaders gained greatly from the workers. Early in the projects, the leaders' contact with the hospitals or welfare workers was sporadic, their knowledge of resources limited, and the range of tenants cared for was a matter of personal bias. Later, their skills and confidence in this area increased greatly. In a positive identification with the worker, they made more effective and sophisticated referrals. They began to work with new agencies, such as housing bureaus, neighboring block associations and churches, in efforts to get services and to change the image of the building in the community.

Yet not all leaders were capable of such far-reaching changes. Since some were themselves often fragile and eccentric, their capacity for change appeared to be limited. They were threatened by changes of behavior in their followers and therefore reinforced the status quo. Thus maladaptive patterns of behavior of individuals became congealed as leader and group approved and supported them.

Sometimes the leaders exerted excessive and arbitrary authority at odds with the goal of sharing and distributing power. Leaders staked out the recreation room as their group's territorial prerogative. Controlling other people's use of it was an extension of their style of leadership in their own "family." Similar problems arose in the handling of other issues.

Control of money for emergency carfare, which had been in the hands of a dominant matriarch, was at issue in this meeting which occurred four months after the beginning of the program.

It was a full hour after the time set before we got the meeting started. Twenty people were present. I said I'd like to go over what we'd discussed at the last meeting, since there were several new people and explain about the carfare. Mug said this was no go, Sugar should keep the money, so I said we'd throw it open to discussion again. Mike and Mug were the ones most interested in having Sugar keep the money. Frank gave concrete reasons why it would be better at the desk, as did several others. Mug maintained it would be easier for Sugar to have it. I said, since there were people of different persuasions, what would they think of keeping $5 at the desk and $5 with Sugar. This was also discussed, but the fact of 24 hours' availability at the desk and the fact that some people didn't know Sugar that well swung opinion to the original decision. Mug turned to Mike and Sugar and said he thought it would be better at the desk. Sugar stayed out of the discussion except to say she had no real opinion and that Frank was talking too much. When it became obvious that everyone wanted money kept at the desk, she said that everyone should keep the room clean too, she was tired of doing it. I asked was she angry because she thought we'd made the wrong decision, and she said no, but because she had to clean up the recreation room herself. I said Sugar had carried a lot of the burden for this; perhaps we should devise a system for cleaning up. People threw out that it was an individual responsibility. . . .

Effectiveness in handling these problems hinged on the worker's capacity to help the leader relinquish her control, which was usually absolute and undisputed, while simultaneously developing new and larger arenas of involvement with the leader. For example, as tenants decided to have the lounge open longer, one leader resisted by refusing to give the key to anyone. As the worker and leader became closer and the leader began to share the worker's goals, both were proud of a senile woman's first visit to the lounge, and the willingness of a frightened isolated girl to shop for flowers for Christmas dinner decorations. The leader began to see her role as enabling others to develop, and that this meant someone else could take over the key and its attendant responsibilities. She then moved on to represent the building in the larger community, dealing with other tenants' associations and even the hospital.

Not all the indigenous leaders were able to create a reliable alliance with the worker. The "mother" of one clique had a constant need for assurance about her value and attractiveness to the group larger than her own "family" and was highly vulnerable to the threat of displacement. Such fragility was not uncommon, yet these leaders were often effective when securely operating within the spheres of their own "family."

Conspicuous problems in the early phase revolved about some workers' desire to help the tenants with group tasks beyond their capacity. Errors of judgment were caused by anxiety in the face of massive pathology and seemingly hopeless reality and also by the unstructured therapeutic role. In the earlier projects, workers struggled with the notion that their purpose was to leave behind a functioning, self-reliant group, and that the group could realistically judge the limits of its own activity. The romanticism and even absurdity of these expectations were at times forcefully demonstrated. Initially, the key to the group's capacity to carry out unfamiliar responsibilities was the strength of their relationship to the worker, and this required his actual presence. Only later could tenants function in more formal groups and activities when he was physically absent. For example, in the planning of a dinner party where the worker's avowed plan was emotional and physical noninvolvement, those who volunteered to take on responsibilities, almost to a man, went on a long binge. A group shopping trip downtown, too, proved to be a disaster, much to another worker's dismay. Money provided for clothing went into bottles of wine, and some of the tenants did not turn up until the next day.

Some intervention and direction by the worker of simple actions were essential to assure that the activities were successfully carried out.

Before the meeting began, I met with the people who were going to go shopping. We drew up a list similar to the one that the group had decided upon at the meeting yesterday. I then asked them if they wanted me to go with them or if they thought that they could handle the whole thing themselves. I asked them this several times and all insisted that I could trust them. I gave them the money, and they went to shop. A little while later, I met one of the people who had gone shopping, Virginia, and she said that they did not have enough money for the food and that they had left it at the supermarket. I said that it seemed to me that I had given them enough money, but she said that it wasn't enough. When we got there, I saw that they had bought more than they really needed, and I said this to them, adding that they could have as much as they could eat but that from the other meetings, if anything, we had had food left over all the time.

Both Jimmy and Virginia said that was what they thought, but that Sarah had insisted that they buy more. Sarah was not in the store at this time, and I asked them if they said anything to Sarah, and they said that they did, but that she did not listen. I asked Jimmy if he said anything and he said that he hadn't. I said that I understood how he must have felt, probably worrying that she would get very angry at him. He said that that was it, that she gets so mad sometimes. I said that I knew that Sarah is a bit bizarre, to say the least, and once she gets angry, she is very uncontrollable. I asked them if they thought that if they both had spoken up that it would have helped, and they both agreed. I told Jimmy that I knew that he had trouble doing that, and he said that he did.

We met Sarah outside and I asked her if she was afraid that we would not have enough food. She said that she wasn't greedy and did not come to the meetings to eat. It was impossible to get a coherent answer from her, but I got Virginia and Jimmy to talk to her and tell her how they felt about the food. I told Sarah that I had talked to them, and they said that they did not want to buy so much because they knew that I would get them more if they needed it. Virginia said that that was right, and that there was no need to get more food, if it would just spoil. Sarah nodded with at least some sign that she understood.

On the other hand, overprotection was also a common error. One worker thought that an initial dinner, planned, cooked and served by tenants for the entire building, might demand more capacity for organization than could be expected of the group at that time, and feared that an early failure might have irreversible effects on their new sense of achievement. However, the tenants went ahead with it. While tempers and confusion ran high on that day, the dinner materialized without her active participation. In another situation, she had unspoken qualms about a spiked punch party. Their awareness of her ambivalence and their support of her in the helper role was neatly summarized during the meeting with the remark, "Don't worry! We can manage it," and they did. These parties were consistently held with great enjoyment and appropriate restraint and the local policeman on occasion joined in as a spectator.

Gradually, a strong, positive relationship between the workers and many of the tenants developed. The tenants became curious about the workers as personalities, were highly observant about their values, strengths and anxieties, and became alternately jealous, competitive, seductive, helpless and manipulative, and above all, eager to please them. To accept and work with this emotional attachment was a continuous and difficult process. There was a tendency on the workers' part to deny its existence at first. For example, when one worker went away at Christmas time and there was simultaneously an outbreak of drinking and fighting in public, the connection between the two events was not recognized by the worker until the tenants pointed it out.

An assumption held by workers in earlier programs was that they would have an initial catalytic effect on tenants, then could increasingly withdraw from formal leadership as the effectiveness and experience of the leaders increased. For a variety of reasons, this hoped-for situation did not materialize. In two buildings, there were no informally dominant individuals strong enough to take on formal leadership. In several others the alliance between subgroup leaders and the worker did not form, and a struggle for power between them developed. In one building with a relatively high degree of social interaction, a succession of leaders emerged as their predecessors were, in turn, hospitalized (TB, cancer, cirrhosis of the liver). Two of them subsequently died. In the building in which the manager was the most authoritarian and punitive, authoritarian leadership styles emerged in the tenants' organization despite efforts by the worker to help the group choose more benign individuals who would foster participation in decision-making and who would promote independence and self-reliance.

In one building in which the worker was able to phase himself out, there were several leaders of different types; as one fell ill, went on a binge, or was out of favor, others took over. Here the worker came to function as a "backstop" in major crises or as a mediator in conflicts between leaders.

The leaders in another building who had assumed responsibility for others were an inexperienced but dedicated triumvirate. They managed to work together despite fierce interpersonal hostilities, punctuated by intermittent crises and realignments—any two of them against the third. One was a Negro woman in her mid-forties with strongly developed social skills. A long-standing alcoholic, she was prone to severe attacks of anxiety and had had one psychiatric hospitalization. She was the conscience and scourge for many tenants, with a punishing tongue and an overt attitude of condescension which masked tenderness and concern. Her position in the building supported her own fragile self-esteem. More than a dozen tenants were profoundly dependent on her, and she was the primary bridge between the manager and the tenants.

The second was a Negro in his middle thirties, an addict since his teens, who had recently given up the drug habit after a long period of incarceration. A gentle, appealing person, he was struggling to find courage to go hunting for a job. He had a gift for comforting others which extended to a belief in his own healing power. He attracted older people to him; they depended on him for medicine and comfort. The third, a former TB patient, was a politically fervent, litigious and suspicious young man who was eminently sensible and task-oriented. He had few personal relationships. However, his respectability and intelligence made him a highly important spokesman.

Supporting these three were others. One, a 240-pound, witty and sarcastic woman was the central feeding figure for a group of addicted men. Her role in meetings was to describe sardonically but affectionately their common skeleton in the closet. She energetically organized a sewing room and helped to teach many tenants to outfit themselves. Another was a tall young man, semi-blind, a veteran with a heart condition. He was the building's best cook and was a reliable mainstay of the dinners which evolved as part of the program. At least one-fifth of the building's population assumed responsibility for others in some form.

"Successful" leaders tended to become upwardly mobile and often moved out of SROs into their own apartments; only a very few, however, became employed. A vexing and unresolved problem arose when leadership was siphoned off in a population so marginal that replacement did not occur.

Group Process in Meetings

Weekly meetings, usually with the serving of food, were held in most projects. The meetings were attended by a quarter to a half of the buildings' population and were chaired by dominant tenants. Usually they started an hour late and people drifted in and out continually. Learning to discuss, to take turns, to dare to differ, to stay with one issue, or to vote, was very difficult for many tenants. In one project, early meetings were characterized by such random and seemingly irrelevant interactions that the worker nearly gave up. However, once people became accustomed to one another and understood the rules of the game, many came to enjoy meetings immensely.

Nevertheless, concepts of self-determination and democratic procedure became ambiguous when applied to a group with a quickly shifting and unstable emotionality and where many individuals were more strongly related to inner feelings than to outer reality. Because of this and the ingrained habit of passivity shown by many tenants, the worker set out to establish an atmosphere of friendly informality in meetings, yet with sufficient order to encourage the timid offer of an opinion or an alternative. The dominant natural leaders tended to encourage the patterns of compliance and found great difficulty in understanding the worker's point of view, being baffled by the worker's opinion that, for example, an argument between usually silent members over black-eyed peas or carrots to be served at a tenant dinner might be as valuable as clear and wise decisions from her. Planning of agendas and teaching techniques of chairing the meetings were major vehicles for transmission of the worker's values. The patterns varied in different projects in this regard.

The workers struggled to avoid the direct control of behavior in meetings, but the way to place responsibility for providing controls was not always clear. In some projects, the workers never chaired meetings. One of them spent regular time teaching group techniques to the eloquent but uninfluential chairman. She often felt troubled about the manipulative aspects of this;

his "How am I doing?" glance left her uncomfortable, yet she saw no alternative. In another building, the worker ran the meetings because the natural leader would not, and there seemed to be no replacement. Later the worker accepted this as an appropriate role for herself. Both approaches enabled the groups to consolidate, to perceive choices, however slowly and painfully, and to make decisions.

Intragroup Tension

Since a common feature of these buildings was a strong in-group feeling among tenants with the same type of pathology, the worker was often called upon to deal with the tensions between such subgroups. The "winos" and "junkies" tended to go their separate ways; there were also a few white downwardly mobile women who were suspicious, mistrustful and hostile to those among whom they lived, creating a black-white schism.

In many projects the lounge became the arena for territorial struggles between the addicts and the alcoholics. The resolutions of these conflicts were intense and sometimes poignant group experiences. The attitudes toward one another were made quite explicit in one project after both alcoholics and addicts became active visitors in the lounge. While contempt was registered on both sides, it was clear that the addicts regarded themselves, and were regarded by the alcoholics, as having greater status. As one of the alcoholics put it, "They have to be smarter than we are," or as an addict asserted, "Winos are just bums with a cheap habit." They became increasingly hostile to each other in one meeting until an addicted woman, silent until then, stated, "What are we all jawing about? We're all in trouble, bad trouble; nobody cares if it's the bottle or the needle, except us." The room was utterly silent; several people quietly began serving cookies and an informal buzz of conversation sprang up. The issue was not brought up at their meetings again in a hostile context.

In another building, a small group of addicts used the recreation room as a shooting gallery, forcing the manager to close the room for a time. The territorial issue was fought out in meetings which concluded with the unenthusiastic agreement that all should use the room.

In one such discussion, a highly eloquent woman addict said, "Everybody here has a hangup; mine is different from yours—no better, no worse; we've got this room—let's not get hung up fighting about who's better, winos or junkies. We'll lose the whole program that way." The deep feelings which surfaced were not so quickly stilled, however.

The following dinner was being cooked by an addict. Some panicky and mistrustful alcoholics decided to boycott the dinner. The worker watched the meal in preparation and casually described what was going on in the kitchen, calling for help with various errands. A family of alcoholics asked the worker earnestly if they could somehow get sick by eating the food being prepared. As the discussion deepened, it was clear that the alcoholics had a profound fear of pollution or infection. The worker pointed this out, and the "mother" said abashedly that it *was* rather silly. By this time, the smells of cooking spaghetti sauce were seeping into the central hallways and spreading in the building. The most vociferous anti-junkies came to the recreation room, ate well and gave the cook the customary ovation of appreciation and goodwill.

The welfare recipients in one of the buildings were felt to be excluding the non-welfare recipients. In another, the Puerto Ricans felt excluded by the Negroes. Among people who were deeply depressed and hopeless, the struggle for possession and control of the recreation room was a major emotional experience which had many constructive elements. Successful bargaining and sharing with the other subgroups was the prototype of many later encounters with hostile outsiders.

But in two buildings, the lounge was successfully pre-empted by an ingroup.

Through the course of the summer, the coffee percolator and the record collection have been stolen and the tenants now fear for the loss of the phonograph and the television as soon as anybody who would steal them is able to line up a buyer. One tenant expressed the fear that the sofa would soon be missing, too. And all of this has happened despite the fact that the room has been kept locked!

The locking of the recreation room has been a source of great contention for the rudimentary tenants organization. The key has been entrusted to three relatively responsible women who, in turn, are in charge of opening the room for other sober, responsible individuals. In theory, this arrangement is supposed to keep the room open from 11 A.M. to 11 P.M. every day of the week. In practice, however, the only times that the room had been unlocked were for the Monday afternoon tenants' organization meetings. Vociferous "out-groupers" have loudly decried the present arrangement for the control of the key at these meetings by asserting that the room is only used to pamper "in-groupers" who are sycophants to the women who control the key.

The fact of the matter is that the "out-groupers" do have a valid point.

I had one occasion to be in the room of one of the women who control the key when an "out-grouper" knocked on the door and asked if he could be admitted to the room. Although he was sober, his request was flatly refused as a matter of principle aimed directly at him. In the screaming which ensued, he (a Puerto Rican) accused her (a Negro) of discrimination and favoritism, while she declared that even though he was sober, he was still not the least bit responsible and she certainly was not about to let him into the room where he could break and steal things. Although they each had large elements of truth in their arguments, she won an almost unanimous 9–1 decision (possession being nine-tenths of the law). The arguments were again repeated at the subsequent tenants' meeting generating anger, slander and curses, but amidst the anarchy, the "out-groupers" proved totally incapable of uniting, and the control of the key remained in the hands in which it had been before, despite the outrage, sulking, and vindictive turmoil. As might have been predicted, the room was open the following day from eleven till eleven with largely "in-groupers" in attendance, and refreshments were served to prove to everybody what a great job the recreation room committee was doing. After that, the room slipped back into its general pattern of disuse because, after all, one of the women who controls the key dislikes TV, the other two have TVs in their own rooms, and all three function in accordance with the building norm of having an extremely small amount of patience for doing something for somebody who is not simultaneously doing something for them.

Conflict and Group Disruption

Verbal abuse, violent acting out and disorganization of individuals occurred fairly frequently, even in group meetings. Early in the development of formal group meetings, indviduals would impose controls on one another in an effort to make a more favorable impression on the worker. Later, the group itself was genuinely irritated by disruptive behavior. A common problem for the worker was that of dealing simultaneously with the reality situation, stimulating group control when necessary, and sensing and making explicit the group's and his own anxiety about control of disruptive behavior.

The group was often unsuccessful in setting and enforcing limits; the worker here intervenes with the disruptive member:

Mrs. Robinson has been creating more and more of a disturbance at the meetings. She is drunk frequently, and constantly breaks into other people's conversations, often with hostility, particularly at today's meetings toward Mr. Clayton, whom she called a liar, irresponsible, and a drunk. The group usually tells her to be quiet, to no avail. In addition, she usually sits near me and constantly seeks my attention. I have tried to explain to her that I can't listen to other people and herself at the same time and to reassure her that she will be heard, etc. During the meeting, I often hold her hand when she seems particularly agitated. This seems to help some. At this last meeting, the group reprimanded her, time and time again, to no avail. I finally said to her, "You know, Mrs. Robinson, if I were a member of this group, I would consider asking you to leave." The group did not pick up on this, and no one suggested that she leave, although she did quiet down some. They tried to control her by asking everyone to raise their hands, and Mrs. Robinson did so persistently and was given the right to speak, but then started interrupting again.

The group is very important to her, as well as my approval and affection and that of other staff members. After the meeting, Mrs. Robinson came over to me and asked me if I were mad at her. I said, "You know that you made it very hard to have a meeting today, because you kept interrupting people and yelling." Mrs. Robinson said she was sorry, she meant well. I put my arm around her and said that I knew she did and I liked her, that perhaps she could control herself better if she didn't drink so much before the meeting. Mrs. Robinson said she had not been drinking. (Her breath reeked of liquor, but there didn't seem to be much point in getting into a battle of wills about it, so I moved on.) I said, "Then I wonder why you were so angry today and didn't seem to be able to control it." Mrs. Robinson said she was just kidding with Mr. Clayton. I said it didn't sound like that to me. She said she just wanted to be helpful, she was trying very hard, but she got carried away.

I said that I guessed the other members knew that she was trying hard to be helpful, since they had not thrown her out of the meeting. Mrs. Robinson said, "But I was a bad girl today, huh?" I said that she had seemed to me as if something was upsetting her. She said no, and added that she would be absolutely quiet at the next meeting. I said that I didn't mean that she should be absolutely quiet —sometimes she had very good ideas, and we wanted to hear them. Mrs. Robinson said, "If you tell me to leave, I will." I said, "Do you want me to help you to control yourself at the meetings?" Mrs. Robinson said that she would try to be quieter. I said, "You know, it seems to me that you are always particularly excited and agitated when there is a committee meeting." Mrs. Robinson said, "My heart and soul are in this." I said that perhaps she worried a lot about the meetings and that was why she was so full of energy at them. Mrs. Robinson said yes, she wanted them to go well. I said, "Would it help if we talked about the meeting a little bit before it started, so you needn't be so nervous?" We arranged next week for us to talk before the meeting.

How drunk an SRO alcoholic acts seems to some degree to be under his control. Workers have often seen loud and/or obscene behavior suddenly disappear under certain circumstances: group disapproval, the worker's arrival, an injury to himself, or some other event of supervening interest or stress. Conversely, people not very drunk have enacted the role of jester or court fool during meetings, and under the guise of intoxication, made incisive and honest comments about the program, the worker, or relationships within the group. While an alcoholic would, when sober, not dare to argue with the manager, he might even rage at him when drunk, apologizing the next morning for his drunken behavior.

Managers, Workers and Tenants: An Uneasy Triple Alliance

As the programs got underway, the managers' tendency to depersonalize the tenants and their difficulty in evaluating their strengths came to the fore. While the worker had a conviction that the tenants were potentially adult, responsible, and able to control their behavior, managers sometimes had the opposite conviction. This counterpoint between optimism and pessimism, hope and despair, democratic and authoritarian styles, occurred with every pair. The following two excerpts illustrate the tension between workers and managers. The first occurred on the morning after the initial unsupervised tenants' party, and was a courteous argument between manager and worker:

Mr. S. began positively, and I knew from past experience that he must be displeased with something. He said that the party last night was super, and when he came in in the morning, he checked the recreation room and it was immaculate. Of course, since I wasn't there, it might have gotten rough; but he would not want me to be going home at such a late hour, any more than he would his mother or daughter. I said that I certainly appreciated his concern about my safety, but that I knew that he must also be concerned about what would happen at the party with no staff person present. He said that that was it, a staff person indirectly "polices" the party. He then told me that beer was served at the party and he did not think this was helpful to people trying to control their alcoholism. I asked if he wanted me to set a rule about beer at parties. He said he did not want to be quoted like that, but that money for food went farther than for beer. I suggested that it be up to a decision the tenants made, provided there was more clarity about planning for the party and responsibility for it. He said that we should see what the hospital's policy would be about buying beer. I said that I would be glad to find out, and that I would be working now with the tenants concerning party planning and would let him know.

In another building, control of the TV set became an issue between worker and manager. The manager's protective and custodial attitudes tended to shortcircuit tenants' efforts to work out their own solution, which if successful, could have begun a group process of increasing control over the violence in the environment and among themselves.

The managers relied on the workers to meet crises both medical and psychiatric. Here is a sad episode:

Mr. K., the manager, called to ask that I come to the building to help with a tenant who was without medication and was highly hysterical. This turned out to be 67-year-old Mr. G., who has TB, cirrhosis of the liver, and is mentally ill. He had run out of Librium, and was very drunk. I also found out that the snow had leaked through the roof and his mattress was wet. As I came to his room, he jumped up and said angrily that I didn't care about him. Then he went into the lobby, shouting a stream of obscenity as I followed.

After screaming and threatening for more than an hour from the stairs, Mr. G. yelled, "Mr. K. [the manager], I wish Hitler had killed all of you Jews, all of you; lined all of you up against the wall; see, he just didn't get all of you." Mr. K. seemed to get redder and redder in the face. Mr. G. then said plaintively, "I need my medicine. I'll go get me another bottle." Mr. K. got very angry, then said to him, "Well, all right, you sucker, you'll have to starve for the next two weeks because I don't intend to give you anything." I got Mr. G. upstairs then, and gave him medication. Later that night, Mr. G. came down to say he was sorry. Mr. K. said, "These things happen. I'm sorry for what I said to you, too."

After a long initial period of caution and mistrust, these managers grew to find the program a positive asset, not only economically for themselves, but emotionally for themselves and for their tenants. After more than six months of programs, two landlords in particular became active participants in extending the groups' opportunities for enjoyment. For example, one offered his own car and his time to drive the tenants when there was a problem of transportation in a baseball excursion. Another, who initially had been extremely mistrustful of tenants to the point that he would not grant them responsibility over the key to the recreation room, conferred a year later with the tenants' steering committee about changes of policy in his intake procedures and went to them for help in solving difficult individual problems of tenants. One manager donated a turkey for a Thanksgiving dinner held by tenants as part of their newly developed tenants' association. However, he refused to admit to the tenants that it was his donation. His comment is ". . . then they'll think they can con me into anything." All but one continued to donate the recreation room space, which was a direct loss in rental income.

In essence, the workers sought to find that delicate balance point between protecting and enabling, between focusing on the pathology and on the strengths, between expecting and encouraging too little or too much change. They struggled to give of themselves consistently and generously to a deprived, profoundly dependent population, while striving to seek out and support the impulses of individuals to take up again the interrupted process of growth toward independence and autonomy. Early signs of initiative, task persistence and completion, work satisfaction, and effective verbal expression of feeling were encouraged. Active mastery and exercise of choice, even if it were merely to resist an impulse to flee a forbidding hospital intake clerk, or to tell one's welfare investigator about the needed winter coat, were recognized, warmly praised and supported, at first by the workers, then by the group.

In these chapters I have traced the content of programs, what tenants and workers did together from their first meetings to termination; I have also tried to capture the quality of the shifting relationships between them and the conflicts they had to resolve together.

5

Connecting Tenants to Services: Referral

> It is a responsibility of the teacher to the student, just as it is of the young doctor to his patient, to inspire the right amount of hope—some, but not too much. Excess of hope is presumption and leads to disaster. Deficiency of hope is despair and leads to decay. Our delicate and precious duty as teachers is to properly tend this flame.
>
> —KARL MENNINGER

Tenant movement toward more effective use of services was conspicuous among two very different parts of the tenant population. At one extreme were the active participants in the program who became strongly involved with the tenants' association and the worker and, through him, moved further into the community. At the other extreme were certain fringe tenants, downwardly mobile individuals with whom the worker established casework relationships, as a result of which it became possible for some of them to accept referrals.

Interest in rehabilitation and referral usually was a sequel to participation in the recreation-lounge program. A shift in the morale of those participating seemed to allow for the emergence of a sense of hope as well as a sense of anger at service institutions. Many tenants were painfully articulate about their lack of success in getting services of any kind. They spoke about intake procedures as being especially frightening and confusing. Some expressed anger at what they felt to be inequality of opportunity for obtaining service. Institutions toward which feelings were highly charged were welfare, police, courts, and hospitals. Hope for oneself and anger toward the outside combined to galvanize the group into a new channel of action. Recognizing that it was a double problem—the fear of referral which led to tenant apathy and the resistance to such clients in the various institutions—the tenants in many buildings appointed committees to cooperate with the worker on case-finding and to help make and meet appointments for all tenants.

The intake process at all institutions reflected nonreciprocal expectations by givers and receivers of services. As an example, admission to an inpatient detoxification unit usually necessitated two visits to the far end of the city and two or more all-day waits. Addicts who lived in terror of experiencing withdrawal symptoms in the waiting room of the hospital were, time after time, unable to face this procedure. Special arrangements for immediate admission at a preplanned time resulted in the rapid hospitalization of seventeen addicted residents of one building in a period of a few weeks, often in small groups on the same day. Again, an extremely shy young man, unable to make himself clearly understood, attempted four times to get on the waiting list of a psychiatric clinic. Each time he had been so overcome with fear and confusion that he left before the intake procedure was completed. When accompanied by another tenant already under treatment, he was able to finish a diagnostic interview.

While one can attribute these incidents to the lack of appropriate self-presentation on the part of the prospective client-patients and to a tacit screening-out process on the part of the service institutions, neither interpretation helps to solve the problem. To bridge the gap in communication, to interpret the institution to the tenants and vice versa, was a major task of the worker and the indigenous leaders.

Liaison was established with two hospitals and a narcotics rehabilitation center. Cooperative working relationships were built with the Department of Social Services, whose social workers had reduced and consolidated case loads in the project buildings. Tenants who wanted support were accompanied to a new clinic or center by another tenant or volunteer, and efforts were made to interest the receiving agency in the projects as a whole. The work of accompanying people after the first months was largely done by tenants, who, while ill themselves and on welfare, devoted hours each day to reminding and encouraging people about appointments, arranging carfare, and sitting in waiting rooms, acting *in loco parentis*.

Referral Outcome in One Project Building

The following table summarizes the number of referrals which took place in one building. The total of sixty-eight represents the number of satisfactory referrals, that is, those which resulted in an ongoing service. Fifty-two individuals, or one-half the building population, were involved. (In many cases, one individual was involved in two or more referrals.)

While in most instances tenants were able to continue contact with the service institutions to which they were referred independently after the first few visits, a few were repeatedly in need of support. One such tenant was a young woman with active TB who, when drunk, could become violent. Every visit by her to psychiatric or medical facilities took endless planning. Another person became disoriented for time and place when drunk; she was repeatedly brought to psychiatric emergency when assaultive, but always managed a sufficiently rational interview to prevent hospitalization or acceptance into treatment.

Those tenants who were the most accepting of referral and were able to follow through were those who took leadership roles. In her study of the population in one project building, Stokes (29) found a direct relationship between tenants' status and acceptance of referral. One tenant leader became steadily employed and entered psychiatric treatment. A second leader vastly reduced her alcoholic intake, entered psychotherapy, and accepted treatment for a chronic medical condition. Two others entered job training programs. In addition to an intermediate group for whom social opportunity combined with referral made a significant change in subjective sense of well-being, there was

TYPE OF SERVICE

REFERRAL SEQUENCE	Dept. of Welfare— New or major changes of old cases	Medical	Detoxification	Psychiatric	Rehabilitation & employment	Total
Protracted procedure; completed service plan	2	4	4	2	3	15
Satisfactory referral procedure; completed service plan	7	21	19	4	2	53
Total	9*	25	23†	6	5	68
Referrals not achieved—no service plan	0	1	2	2	3	8
Referral procedure interrupted—no service plan	1	7	6	2	0	16
Total	1	8	8	4	3	24

* Four of these were new cases opened, two were cases closed.
† Sixteen individuals were detoxified with a completed course; several tenants had two to three courses. Six left the hospital without medical permission.

a large group whose lives were unchanged except for access to the recreation room with its concomitant social relationship.

Referrals for Alcoholism

Attempts at referral to A.A. were made, mainly in the group setting. *In no case* among the five to six hundred alcoholics in all buildings were these efforts successful. However, there is positive evidence that the amount of alcohol consumed was substantially less and that the binge-recovery rhythm of many alcoholics was changed. It was replaced by a pattern of chronic heavy tippling. Damage caused by explosive actions of alcoholics during binges was also markedly reduced. Because of this, check day, traditionally a day for widespread binges, became in time indistinguishable from other days.

This raises the question of the legitimacy of any rehabilitation pattern demanding, as its first step, sobriety for this group. In the inner experiences of the alcoholics in SROs, this is not dissimilar from asking the person with a street phobia to come alone to the psychiatrist, or the insomniac to get a good night's sleep before beginning treatment. For in depriving the SRO alcoholic of wine, we are asking him to shed his primary way of defending himself against a living situation that is intolerable, and to experience, without the blurred denial drink provides, the fear of his death. As Eugene O'Neill expressed it in *The Iceman Cometh:*

I'm afraid to live, am I?—and even more afraid to die! So I sit here, with my pride drowned on the bottom of a bottle, keeping drunk so I won't see myself shaking in my britches with fright, or hear myself whining and praying: Beloved Christ, let me live a little longer at any price! If it's only for a few days more, or a few hours, even, have mercy, Almighty God, and let me still clutch greedily to my yellow heart this sweet treasure, this jewel beyond price, the dirty, stinking bit of withered old flesh which is my beautiful little life.

Both A.A. and the Mission Society approaches to alcoholism appear to be highly unappealing to this group of alcoholics for whom life in sobriety can promise neither family, job nor friends. Stone (30) points out the resistance to A.A. by indigenous lower-class alcoholics. Jellinek (6) also notes that the A.A. value system is profoundly Anglo-Saxon in its orientation. Casual observation of the A.A. alcoholic group suggests that most members would be classified, prior to the alcoholism, as lower-middle or upper-lower class. They are that strata which presumably have the greatest stake in their social status. They have the most to lose.

On New York's Skid Row, the Bowery, the mutual antagonism between the alcoholics and the Mission staffs has been carefully described by Wallace (31). Those who use missions regularly for food and shelter are known in Bowery society as "mission stiffs." They are outcasts; lower on the status hierarchy they cannot go. They have failed not only in the larger world uptown, but have also failed to uphold the values of independence and solidarity of the bottle gang, who view the exchange of the humiliating lip service of religious observance for food as the ultimate in degradation.

The secondary pleasures and the anesthetic effect of chronic tippling is a marginal but workable answer for the fragile SRO population for which the society at this time has no other solutions. The workers, abandoning sobriety as an ideal, were able to become intimate with the alcoholics. The resulting relative sobriety was a by-product of increased self-esteem, not an end in itself.

As part of the intervention, workers often tried to get medical care for alcoholics; the resistance on the part of most hospitals to these potential patients with whom they worked was profound. At one hospital, a guard was stationed at the door who turned away anyone faintly smelling of alcohol. If that barrier were breached, the clerk, the resident or the attending physician would screen out the potential patient. The workers had repeated experiences of this kind, witnessing the return of these patients to the SROs to die.

One worker reported that over a period of four days, he tried to get medical care for a fifty-eight-year-old Negro male alcoholic who was extremely emaciated and was bleeding continuously from the mouth, nose and rectum. At three different hospitals, he used formal and informal channels to get services of any kind without success. On the fifth day, the man died in his SRO room.

Referrals for Addiction

Heroin addicts account for 10 to 20 percent of the SRO population. As a group, they are younger than the alcoholics and are predominantly male and Negro, with a scattering of whites and Puerto Ricans. Their length of residence is shorter than the alcoholics' in part due to police surveillance, in part to the less strong ties with each other. However, as a group, the addicts are by no means solitary; they know one another well, and know other tenants at least by name. Sometimes they shoot together and get a "bag" for one another. The close, dependable ties are between couples, in which the woman is often a prostitute whose "take" supports the habit of both partners. Nevertheless, as a group their relatedness has a temporary, shallow quality, with easily sifting friendships and disrupted rivalries, jealousies and suspicion toward each other. The system of mutual aid, so well-developed among alcoholics, is present but much less dependable, and the network of those who will help one another is smaller.

Addicts are conspicuously different in appearance and manner from other tenants. They are often physically attractive and are sharp dressers. Among the men are natty "cool cats" who are by reputation extremely tidy and clean. Bright, well-pressed clothes, high-fashion shoes and hats are the rule. They seem self-assured and highly verbal in the tenants' group. The educational and work background tends to be of a much higher level than that of the alcoholics; among the addicts whom workers came to know well were many who had formerly been plumbers, masons, chefs and musicians. A few had been to college; one had dropped out as a medical student. There were a handful who had been or still were con men; minor pushers, past and present, had very high status among the addicts and were often addressed as "Mister" or by last names only. One man who said he had run a chain of brothels at one time was now a minor pusher. He was respected by most, feared by some; people sought his advice because they felt he could successfully maneuver in the world, and indeed he could be extremely helpful.

In the tenants' organization, he spoke little, sat aloof, dignified and immaculate, registering his opinion or throwing his weight in behind-the-scenes, through informal channels. It took the worker in this building a very long time to recognize his power and form an alliance with him.

In those buildings with close social networks, there existed an understanding that the addict would not steal in his own building. Where people were less closely connected, addicts preyed regularly on elderly and, especially, alcoholic tenants. In one building, a single addict, a forty-year-old Italian-American who was formerly a contractor and who had an extremely heavy habit, begged, borrowed and, when desperate, stole. A work injury involving his arm and back had made him semicrippled and in chronic pain. He was held in the greatest contempt by the tenants, addicts and nonaddicts alike.

A medical student, observing an SRO during the summer, developed a close bond with an addict. He described him in the following report:

Billy was a 19-year-old heroin addict. In spite of the fact that he earnestly was anxious to cooperate with me in completing a questionnaire, he had extreme difficulty sitting very long in one place without getting highly agitated. Apologizing for his actions, Billy would jump up and run away begging me to stay just a little while until he returned. (And the "while" often turned out not to be so little.) His embarrassment with having to leave me was balanced against his desire to have me coming many times to see him. Each time he made me promise to come back because he said he had never had a friend he could talk to before. He said that many of the things we talked about when we were together made him sad and made him realize unpleasant things about the way he was throwing his life away. He was convinced that talking to me was making him change. He said that talking with me (I didn't do much more than just listen) made him realize that he should do something more with the second half of his life than with the first. (The fact that a person such as I, untrained, should be able to draw a response such as this from a person who hadn't asked to see me in the first place after a total of only a couple of hours talking, is plainly frightening.) . . . And Billy unashamedly said that he was anxious to drag out our interview as long as possible so that he could talk to me as much as he possibly could. Even when I was leaving the building at the end of my study, he made me promise that if I were ever to come back, I would stop at his room and see him to talk some more. This last item more than any other convinced me that at least a large part of what Billy had been telling me was sincere, and that this wasn't just a case of someone who was getting ready to try to beg me out of some money and had gotten carried away with his own oratory.

Billy also showed several instances of basic trust for me. One day he showed me the costume jewelry he had stolen from a drugstore that morning to help finance his habit, lamenting that it was worth only about six dollars, but if he had been caught, it would have netted him six months in jail. He also showed me his syringe and the place on his arm where he had misinjected himself the night before and caused a puffy, swollen spot. But all this didn't serve to make it easier to continue talking to him when he began to get agitated. On two occasions, I got up with him, at his own suggestion, and we went for a walk down the street as we talked. But even then, both times his agitation continued to grow until we had to break off the interview anyway. There wasn't a single time we talked that it wasn't a race against time to see how far we could get through the interview before we would have to stop again. Although there were no questions asked about it in the interview schedule, Billy freely described himself to me as being sexually frustrated, and this sexual hangup became evident in other activities during our interviews as well. Once when we were sitting on the front step, Billy looked down to the corner and saw a prostitute walking past. He jumped up and ran down the street to catch her without even bothering to finish the sentence he was saying to me. Another time in the middle of one of our conversations, he spontaneously began to masterbate. But on a third occasion, he was protective of my sensitivities. He was sitting with me in his room with a man and a woman friend when another one of his friends came in with a girl friend. Billy then politely asked me to leave and stand in the hall for a little until we could talk some more because he thought the second friend was getting ready to have relations with the girl.

In all project buildings, some of the addicts came to like and trust the workers and to ask for help in getting detoxification. This was usually not with a view to becoming "clean"—for this group, such a goal was remote, though sometimes feigned for the service professions involved with them. Rather, periodic detoxification reduces the amount of heroin necessary. When a man needs five to ten "bags" a day at an average of $5.00 a bag, it becomes an exhausting feat to steal this much. Goods have to be converted into money, then the pusher, sometimes local, sometimes in a distant neighborhood, has to be found and bargained with; time must be made to shoot and enjoy the afterglow—not to speak of eating, sleeping, shopping and socializing. SRO addicts, in contrast to alcoholics, were busy, pressed for time, always in a hurry, slipping in and out of their groups in their perpetual hunt for money and heroin.

Thus the addicts, as they became increasingly burdened, would try to get into one of three detoxification hospitals. The timing was crucial; check day was best, as rent could be paid for the two weeks when an addict would be away, and his status would remain unchanged. He could then return on the next check day to pay his rent again and resume his life with a "light" habit. Policies regarding addicts on welfare differ from center to center and investigator to investigator. One possibility is that he may be dropped off the rolls, which he can ill afford, if his investigator finds out; or another investigator may be helpful in getting him into a hospital and may try to find post-hospital care and training for him. The hospital worker, not having the burden of financial complications of this sort, is at an advantage in developing a relationship with the addict.

The workers cultivated channels of intake into the three hospitals which bypassed the one- to two-day waiting room sequence that involved such overwhelming anxiety and physical suffering for the addict going into withdrawal. When SRO addicts came to understand that this uncertain wait could be avoided, many gratefully accepted referrals. In one building, all 18 addicts with one exception were hospitalized in a period of six weeks. They planned with the worker on the date and the friend with whom they would be going. Then they put aside one "bag" for the early morning of that day. At 6:00 A.M. they would awaken each other, have their "fix" and be in the lobby by 7:30, where the worker would meet them, having pre-arranged with the hospital intake worker to reserve beds. They went by taxi to the hospital and were admitted by 8:30. It became a standing joke among the addicts that they were all going to be "fixed" up. Tenants wrote to those in the hospital, sent money for cigarettes and telephone calls. They were welcomed back as heroes.

Many of the women addicts had children in foster placement, and it was a recurrent daydream to become "clean" and get the children back. One woman, with two older children in placement and a two-year-old with her, wanted to go to the hospital but did not dare lest the investigator find out and have this child removed. She was finally picked up for prostitution and the child was taken from her anyway. The mother grieved for months. Two years later, she died of an overdose.

In a building where many addicts had been detoxified as part of the program, the following incident took place:

One man, though friendly, was secretive and denied his habit. He tried to beg the worker for money for a "bag" which he knew she could not give him. During a meeting held in a tenant's room, he sat next to the worker on the bed. Her purse was behind her. She felt the purse being jiggled and as she unobtrusively reached behind her, found his hand in her purse. She closed her hand over his and held it quietly and firmly for several minutes inside the purse. He did not move, but reddened and withdrew from the discussion. No one in the room noticed. Later, he slipped out and became withdrawn for many days. He finally apologized simply and seemed more shaken by the worker's behavior than his own. He was then able to talk about his addiction but was not interested in detoxification. He died a year later; it was said that he was in a knife fight with a pusher.

Other Referrals

Casework with individual tenants who did not necessarily participate in the program also resulted in referrals. These tenants often required very practical help: making telephone calls and appointments, working through the fear of a necessary hospitalization, finding relatives, and changing of rooms or housing.

There were in every building elderly, family-less white people who had become stranded by poverty and age in the same neighborhoods where they had grown up. Irish, Italian and Jewish, they had been left behind as their ethnic groups moved out to the suburbs. Most had lived in their present SROs for at least ten years, several for as long as twenty-five. They kept aloof from all other tenants and slowly were sinking into senility and physical weakness. A few were religious recluses. One believed that Jesus lived with her. Another had kept all her belongings from a past life in the theater, and her tiny room was stacked to the ceiling with cartons of mementos. Yet another was a ragpicker, making daily rounds of trash baskets for food or usable items.

Some of the socially isolated women had animals which had become the absorbing interest in their lives. Several had refused inhospital treatment for serious conditions because they could not leave their pets and would not allow others to take care of them. More bizarre and pathetic situations were common. One middle-aged white woman, with a long history of mental illness, peopled her small room with dozens of cats; the resulting filth and stench was an insoluble problem to tenants, manager and worker alike. All recognized that the thin thread of sanity hung on the cats. She was persuaded, after many months of work on the worker's part, to lessen the population to four and permitted some help with housekeeping. But the "Cat-Lady" was an ongoing legend in the building, pitied and avoided by others. Another woman, a Negro alcoholic, physically ravaged by disease and drink, had an equally ravaged dog, mangy, half-blind and lame. It was a common sight to see the pair of them very slowly shuffling along, rarely out of touch with each other.

The last bastion of self-respect for the isolated white tenants, the most socially deprived of all the SRO tenants, was their claim to respectability. A boast of frugality, the denial of loneliness, and a harping racial hatred were characteristic of them. Yet, curiously, when given the opportunity to move into a white

SRO, they actually refused. Their identity seemed to have been built on invidious comparisons, a life spun out in clinging to the past, without present pleasure or company.

Much individual casework involved these and other aged and lonely women, some of whom were physically shut in, some approaching senility, yet surviving in the SRO world. In many of these situations, the worker was unable to refer tenants to other services. Institutionalization was a grim last resort, and that too was often unavailable. The frustration of being unable to help beyond offering the comfort of company burdened the workers.

As I was coming into the building, I met an elderly woman (Mrs. F.) who was sitting on the steps between the inside and outside doors. I said hello and asked if she were waiting to go in or just resting. She said that she was on her way out and was resting. I told her who I was, and invited her to the meeting. She said that would be nice and she might come. I asked if I could help her. She told me a story about a terribly fat man on the subway. I asked her how that was related to her. She said that he had fallen on top of her and that had taken the wind out of her for several days. I asked if she were afraid something like that might happen whenever she went out. She said that she was, that sometimes she even had a policeman bring her home because she got so scared coming down the hill. I said that must be dreadful, and she said that she wasn't doing too bad for 71. She began to ramble, and I asked if I could do anything to help her now. She nodded. I asked if she could tell me what it was. She hesitated. I asked if she wanted to wait until after the meeting when I would walk her up to Nedicks where she was going, or if she wanted to get someone to go with her now. She said that she would wait for me until later.

I asked if there were something else that I had not suggested that was bothering her. She said there was not, and that I was a lovely person for offering to help her, and she did not know if I were an investigator, but if so, I was not a usual one. I said that I was not, and that I was here in the building (this I had told her in the beginning) to help the tenants with whatever problems they wanted to work on, and that I thought her difficulty in going out was one such problem. She said that it sure was, and that she was glad I was here.

We started into the building, she leaning on my arm. As we went into the lobby, the manager came out yelling to let go of her, that she was crawling with bugs, and was crazy, and that I couldn't help her, he couldn't help her, she was beyond all help, etc. I started, since I cannot bear little bugs, but I hung onto her, or rather she hung onto me anyway. He went on yelling, and I said that I wanted to help if I could and I had to talk to her to find out. He kept saying I should not talk to her.

We were heading toward the recreation room, and Jackie shook her head at me. The manager said that everyone would have bugs, and I would have bedbugs all over me this very minute, and that I could not take her into the room, etc. I asked Mrs. F. what she had to say about all this. She accused the manager of all kinds of things, and that she had no business being among all these terrible people because she used to work for Mr. Dumpson of D.S.S., etc. I said that I knew she must feel terrible to be talked to like this.

After she left, I went back to Mr. S. and said that I could see what a problem she was to him, and that I hoped it did not seem a put-down to him that I wanted to try to help. He said that I was perfectly entitled to try, but he knew what would happen. I said that he might be absolutely right, but it was my job to try myself, no matter what. He said that he could understand that; I said that it must be sort of annoying when he was saying that he knew best about this woman, and he did have lots of experience with her, and here I come saying that I wanted to see what I could do. He repeated that I sure could try, he did not care, and went on about the horrid state she is in and the way that she is just marking time to die; that she will, if she does not get better care as she would in a home.

That the manager's remarks disturbed the worker's emerging rapport with her future client is indicated in her subsequent reflections on the encounter with Mrs. F.:

She did not respond directly about the bugs at any time, and I did not pursue it to get her ideas about it. At the time whenever Mr. S. mentioned them, she looked at him disdainfully. However, the bugs were in fact crawling on her, so I think I should have made more of an attempt to confront her about it, why she let this happen.

I do not know what I should have done to bring her into the group and let them decide whether or not she was not to be allowed in the group. At the time it seemed too cruel, that the others would feel as Jackie did, that she would just spread the bedbugs around in the recreation room, and she would be chased out. Now I am not sure. I am not exaggerating about the bugs; they were crawling all over her and would in fact have gotten all over the other room. It would not make sense for her to go there in her present state. However, I feel that I was accepting her pariah position too readily.

When I see her, I will try to find out more about why she will not let anyone clean her room and about going to a nursing home or to another hotel.

I am at a loss to deal with a personal part of the situation: I get an allergic reaction to the bedbug bites and I really do not want to catch any. I didn't think about that at the time, but now planning to see her again, I feel hesitant. I expect to tell her that it makes it very hard to help her, but somehow I don't think that is really enough. I have to somehow let her know that it is the bugs, not her. Yet the problem is how to help her do something about the bugs, which must have some bigger feeling behind it besides not knowing how to get rid of them.

The worker was not able to find a way to be helpful. Six months later Mrs. F. was dead.

The presence of the workers stimulated a great many referrals. Most tenants were able to handle them with encouragement from the worker and help from fellow tenants. The contagion of one successful referral experience leading to another and the passage of know-how about resources from tenant to tenant encouraged some tenants to reach out for services they sorely needed.

The process of referral grew along two separate lines, both of which were initially stimulated by the workers' interest and skill. First, those within the network of tenants close to the evolving group program tended to be steered toward agencies by other tenants, with guidance from the worker; they were also urged and supported in this effort by the whole group. Second, those tenants isolated from the program's development tended to create casework relationships with the worker, sometimes accepting referral on the basis of this relationship. In either case, active intervention with the receiving agency—hospital, family agency, court, welfare—was crucial in effecting a "take" in the referral.

6

Endings: Relocation and Separation

> When our worker was leaving, she cried. I was shook up. I was sure then that she cared more than I ever dreamed anyone could care about people like us.
>
> —SRO Tenant

If the relationship to the worker is the hidden key to setting in action a program and the accompanying changes in behavior, how is successful weaning to be accomplished, if at all? Is it ethical to involve a group in so intense an emotional experience that the loss of the worker may leave them once again bereft and emotionally starved, perhaps more hurt and cautious than before?

Our experience in the nine projects offers some leads toward answering these questions, through the examination of the quality of the tenants' experience in the closing phases of the projects and their capacity to replace one worker by another.

Termination by design occurred only in the first building where a six-month interagency exploration took place (16). Two additional projects ended with relocation and follow-up in buildings which were razed by their owners; the decisions to do so were beyond the control of the project workers. Sponsorship of projects in the remaining six buildings was shifted to D.S.S., with on-going training and part-time auxiliary workers continuously provided by the hospital.

Relocation

It is well known that, faced with removal, SRO tenants—
having comparatively weak neighborhood roots and few possessions—simply disappear.

A Site Management Report for 1961 of the N.Y.C. Housing
Authority (27) reported the relocation pattern in 15 SRO
buildings. Of a total of 632 SRO tenants subject to relocation,
47 went into public housing, 87 into other apartments, 23 into
the rehabilitated buildings; seven were institutionalized or died.
". . . The remaining 234 tenants consisted largely of single persons under 60 who were not eligible for any bonus payments
and whose new housing was therefore not inspected. Many of
these single persons moved to 'address unknown.' "

Two project SROs where relocation took place were owned by
institutions. Both had evolved well-developed programs in a
variety of activities with a high degree of tenant participation.
A palpable shift in atmosphere had occurred in the buildings.
Relocation in both instances was experienced and worked
through as a group problem.

By the time that the initial program was begun in the first
building, it had long been the object of strong community pressure because of its notoriety. Public disturbance and antisocial
behavior had all but disappeared during the latter phase of the
program. The decision to relocate the tenants from the structurally unsound building was announced by its owners after
acquisition of the lease in the fifth month of the program; the
tenants were reassured about having enough time and help with
relocation from management. The tenants nevertheless reacted
to the relocation announcement with marked anxiety. Some
wanted to retain a lawyer and fight relocation. Others, fearing
that a court decision favoring the tenants against the owners
was highly unlikely, felt that engaging in a hopeless legal fight
would only sacrifice the positive aspects of planned relocation.
Some were incredulous about the owners' stated intentions to
pursue an individualized constructive relocation plan. Still others
saw relocation as a potentially positive change. The leadership

of the building was evenly split, for and against litigation. Two weeks of incessant discussion throughout the building ended in a vote of six-to-four in favor of open cooperation with relocation efforts. The worker herself was ambivalent on the issue; the tenants were obviously no longer a social menace to the community; on the other hand, a building already badly deteriorated would not provide adequate housing much longer, no matter how positive its internal social environment had become. The worker did not take part in the decision-making process.

The tenants' association was invited by management to participate in relocation planning, and a relocation committee was formed. Tenants and owners, in a series of meetings, sought to determine the details of the relocation process. The following joint decisions were arrived at: Wherever possible, friendship groups or pairs should be relocated together; new housing must be at least equivalent to and preferably better than current housing; financial aid would be given by management for moving and other expenses due to relocation such as down payments on apartments; no tenant should move without an opportunity to explore some of his major problems with a social worker who was to be hired by management for this purpose; tenants who would prefer to move to an apartment instead of a furnished room would be helped to do so; and those who were most physically and emotionally ill would be moved first and with greatest attention.

The total process of relocating slightly more than one hundred people took about six months. About one-third of the tenants found new quarters on their own. The balance were helped to do so by the new manager, hired by the institutional owners to empty the building. Throughout this period, the Department of Social Services (D.S.S.) worked closely with the manager to effect smooth relocation.

The manager became a pivotal person soon after he arrived during the fifth month of the program. His combined qualities of firmness ("Notice: Any tenant throwing garbage out of the window risks eviction") and concrete helpfulness with everyday urgent needs helped to calm the whole population. He locked the front door and provided twenty-four-hour watchman service, and also improved cleaning and maintenance services. He came to know most of the tenants as individuals. During relocation, he took tenants to see alternative rooms or apartments and helped them to move their belongings. The building owners donated the furniture in the building to the tenants; some took enough repaired and painted pieces to furnish their new apartments. A clothing drive by community church groups during the fall assured each tenant of winter clothing.

Of the one hundred tenants, less than 5 percent elected to move away from Manhattan's upper West Side. Seventeen were relocated in eight apartments of two rooms or more. The remainder relocated in other SRO buildings. Nine tenants moved together to one such building and combinations of two, three and four tenants moved to a series of others. Only two individuals chose to live in SROs considered physically or socially marginal despite attempts at dissuasion.

The following excerpts from a New York *Times* article on November 3, 1965, concern the attitudes of tenants toward their relocation:

... A recent survey of some of the new rooms and apartments found by Mr. C. disclosed a dramatic improvement in living conditions.

"Oh, Christ, you can escape," said Mary P., when asked about her new three-and-a-half room apartment at — West 110th Street. "You're not like cluttered together. You can go into the kitchen, go into the living room. We've got a parlor, as they say."

Mrs. P. and her roommate, Mrs. Florence S., had been paying $138 a month for two rooms at the B. (hotel). Their new rent is $95 a month.

Seven tenants moved into a clean, orderly building at — West 94th Street, where the manager, ———, says he can "spot an addict and have him out the day he moved in."

One couple, Mr. and Mrs. Henry S., who had two rooms at the B. (hotel) for $133.66 a month, now have a three-and-a-half-room apartment at — West 109th Street for $87 a month.

Most of the tenants wanted to remain on Manhattan's West Side.

"I think everybody's very happy. Half of them have stopped drinking, no joke," Mrs. P. said of the other tenants.

Mrs. S. said: "They got better places than what they had. Mr. C. took them around and they picked their own place."

This is a leading tenant's version of the relocation as it affected her:

In the latter part of July, five tenants met with the educational institution which owns the building to try to decide which way was better for relocation. Since we had so many older and sick people, it was decided that we start in August while it was warm. The tenants were taken around in cars to decide where they wanted to live. We were allowed to paint and have all the furniture. With different community groups, we got housekeeping materials and clothes. Some got apartments, and everyone received money to give them a headstart toward rehabilitation. Everyone came daily to the recreational room and dinners and meetings which went on, although we were moving. I felt sad at times, but the building was unable to be repaired with anyone in it.

At one of the meetings, I decided I would be one of the last tenants to move, so if a tenant had a problem, I could be there to discuss it with them and the proper persons. One day Ann [the worker] and I looked at rooms and apartments. Either the rent was too expensive, or I disliked them. Then, with the help of the institutions, I saw my present apartment and was very pleased with it and decided that it held everything I wanted and how it could be made into a home.

I took all the furniture I needed from the old building and a couch was donated for my living room. I received linens, curtains and all the household equipment that is needed to furnish three rooms, including a private bath.

I was moved by station wagon with two trips and that was paid for by Welfare.

My present building is different from the old building in this respect: I have a locked door with an intercom system and no one can gain entrance without my knowledge of who the person is. My apartment is very cheerful, and there is sufficient space to play the TV, read, or just relax. My apartment is so comfortable, that I look forward to going home and doing different little things in it.

After relocation the majority of the tenants continued to meet weekly in the empty building. Then space was found in a centrally located church where semimonthly dinners were held by the tenants' association. Half the tenants lost touch altogether with the association at this point. Many poignantly expressed the loss of friendships and familiar patterns established in the building. However, the core group continued to meet for the next year. On the whole, they were able to maintain the level of adaptation achieved during the program. Those who began working continue to do so. Those whose alcoholic intake had become less remained at the reduced level. However, the addicts as a group did not retain any improvement. Most of those who had become detoxified and managed to stay "clean" have become readdicted and have not returned to the hospital for detoxification.

The nine tenants who were relocated together in one building gradually began a program of their own with Community Psychiatry staff help. Relocated tenants in other buildings, though offered this option in their own buildings, did not follow up.

At this writing, two years after relocation, one-third of the original tenant group continues to be in touch with each other. That they come in any weather and enjoy a meal and each other's company is in itself an important achievement for people whose time sense is vague and spatial mobility limited. These thirty-five tenants are also living in appreciably better housing, and all but one are acceptable tenants where they now live.

The second building to close, which was very similar in population, had a different program history. There, the worker had begun to organize a tenants' association when the building was sold to an institution. Though the institution bought it for its own eventual use, it hoped to continue to operate the SRO for the present tenants for some time. Careful engineering studies of the building, however, showed that it was unsafe. The tenants, therefore, had to move as soon as possible for their own protection. Renovation was out of the question because the beams were so weak that the bathtubs were sinking through the floors to the story below. The institution, concerned about the welfare of the tenants, and in cooperation with the social worker, planned to seek new homes of a type and location they would prefer. Again, tenants were encouraged to move by cliques, with close friends, into new buildings.

The following record shows the worker carrying the news of relocation, which disturbed and disappointed her deeply. It illustrates the difficulty many of the tenants had in expressing their feelings and their passivity in the face of the move:

Relocation Meeting

I went directly to Sugar's [the tenants' association leader] room; Mug was there and was soon joined by Sugar, Victor and Bill. I said I'd heard that they'd heard rumors over the weekend about the building closing. They said they'd been hearing rumors since March, June, etc. I said I wanted them to have facts—the rumors were true, the building was going to have to close. They nodded. I explained about the engineers' report and why the decision was made. There wasn't much response, so I asked what they were thinking and feeling. They just shrugged and asked concrete questions—would they get payments, when did they have to be out—which I answered. I said it was hard news to hear and I wanted them to know what the hospital's thinking was; that they had the right to go to a good or a better building, had the right to move with their friends, stick together, and that we hoped there would be programs in the building to which they moved and that we could start a program. There were several remarks that sounded like o.k. I said I sure wished they'd let me know more what their reactions were and asked Sugar specifically to let me know. She said she'd known this all along.

I said, "You mean you're just glad to have it settled," and she nodded. I said I would like for them to tell me what they felt about my telling the others. It was not easy news to hear and perhaps they had suggestions. Mug said, "Tell them just like you told us." I suggested we get down to the recreation room for the dinner then.

There were about ten people there when we arrived and I went to sit with them, while those I'd already told went to the kitchen or milled around. I approached it in the same manner, starting with the rumor and giving the facts, asking for reactions and giving concrete explanations. I was quite surprised that reactions weren't more visible and weren't angry. Rather, it was a quiet digestion of the facts.

John sent people to knock on doors and people drifted in in twos and threes. I started at the beginning with each new arrival and some had known for an hour or so; the reactions became more visible. Flick and Crewcut cried and I reflected that Flick had been in the building fourteen years; I knew he was feeling more than some of the others. Crewcut cried out in answer to the moving plans, "You mean they're not going to throw us out in the street?" I said, "Of course not"—they couldn't move till they had a place to move to, and he repeated his question several times for confirmation. His tears were of relief at being protected in the move as much as sadness.

People began to shout out places they heard about and would like to move to which John and I wrote down. Sugar and Judy started serving food. As more people came, those who sat near would call to me to tell them about moving. We talked about the food, I answered questions, and then had the chance to move around and talk to individuals: Bill, who has moved three times in the last year; Tony, who's never lived in such a nice place, said I'd upset him so much he couldn't eat. I found myself nodding in answer to people's reactions and touching them or offering them more food. What can you say to someone who has to move and you had to tell them?

The discussion moved from individuals to group attention and Charlie headed the group in response to my question: Weren't they mad? They didn't seem to be. He said there was no use getting mad, he knew about the bathrooms, he remembered when they'd told the manager to fix them and he'd just put up new plaster.

I did offer people the right to see the engineers' report or the pictures of the bathrooms, but they responded by saying they'd seen the bathrooms, they knew what they looked like.

We went over the discussions again and again for three or four hours and I asked, as people started to drift off, if they didn't think it'd be a good idea to have another meeting soon as there was a lot to discuss and also they'd want to report back after they'd had a chance to talk with friends and figure with whom they'd like to move. We planned a menu and set the time. Mug asked would this be another meeting to talk about how they were feeling again and I said yes.

Here, too, relocation with staff help was an optimal time of intervention for many SRO tenants. Choosing location, type of living unit and building (limited as the choice was), and with whom one might want to move, often was highly fruitful. The incredible experience of choice was unfamiliar; at first the tenants in the two buildings with planned relocation did not believe it. Most wanted very modest changes. The preference for SRO-living over apartment-living was very conspicuous. Only three tenants in the first building and two in the second wanted apartments. Others wanted other SROs where programs could be initiated or were already in action.

The relocation also unsettled the isolates and made it possible for the social worker to make contact and provide them with concrete services. This was then the opening to referral for medical care or hospitalization.

For the few senile recluses who managed to survive in the SRO, relocation was a terror which forced them further into illness. There then followed the painful decision to institutionalize them forcibly or finally to evict them.

Other tenants too reacted to the stress of relocation poorly. Whatever the pathology—alcoholic bouts, fighting, withdrawal, decompensation—it became more apparent after the move.

In the remaining six buildings, terminations, separations, and replacement of workers were a common experience for tenants because of the temporary nature of much of the staff—social work students in field placement, summer students, part-time community workers. Only in the first two buildings were trained social workers used. With the foreknowledge that their stay was brief (three to nine months), workers also were affected by the shadow of termination. In almost all projects, nevertheless, intense affection between a core of tenants and the worker and deep commitment to program developed. The stress of separation was thus universally experienced.

Social workers in training were helped in supervision to prepare tenants for this from the beginning, to help them express and work out their anger toward the worker and to help them mourn. This was an exceedingly difficult and sensitive task, made more so by the workers' own anxiety and guilt toward the tenants for having stimulated and gratified dependency needs.

Workers doubted themselves and feared the intensity of their reactions, only later to understand that for themselves and for the tenants "It is better to have loved and lost, than never to have loved at all." Often they struggled with a sense of having to abandon the tenants and were angry at the hospital for not being able to provide new workers immediately. This over-reaction could be seen in a tendency of workers to hold onto some of their responsibility and leadership roles. Some of the tenant leaders could probably have been weaned earlier to assume responsibility but, for example, a student-worker persisted in controlling the program money and chairing meetings. The lesson that one is dispensable was very difficult to master. The worker's struggle with the two opposing views of the client, as infant and adult, gained additional vivid expression in the closing phase. Ideally, the separation could become a new and vigorous challenge to the group toward autonomy; this in fact did take place in several of the buildings but, with one exception, workers left with despair and guilt.

The tenants have had lifelong experience with separation, and the departure of the worker was handled by them somewhat more easily, or at least more briefly, than by the worker. The tenants, after all, were still together, while the worker left into an emotional vacuum. This is a record of a social work student who was about to graduate and go on to a professional job:

I began to mention my departure date. Tenants' conversation was concrete, yet affectionate: "Where are you going?" Someone jokingly commented, "Well, I'm just a baby; I'm just a baby; I'll come to a child welfare agency to see you." "We'll miss you; you're 100 percent—no one can fill your shoes." Questions were immediately forthcoming on who the new worker would be. I answered concretely but used this as a way to elicit from the group their feelings about me. They felt that I had been helpful because I didn't look down on them; I treated them like adults and let them make their own decisions. They felt a male worker would be authoritarian. But they were concerned about losing a "mothering" type of person.

Feelings of rejection or anger were not expressed by the group, although I suggested they might. I gave them an indirect object for their anger in the form of the "impersonal" hospital who had given them three different workers in the first year. They still denied any anger.

It was quite common throughout this last month for the tenants to "forget" the time when I would be leaving, although plans were obviously being made for an elaborate going-away party.

I also began discussion, although hesitantly, about the roles of the tenant leaders and the new worker, who would act more as a consultant-supervisor to the tenants than as an integral part of the group. The main tenant leader felt nervous at new responsibilities, such as full responsibility for the recreation part of the program, but felt she could handle it. A second leader vied for a share in the new responsibility-power and spoke against the main leader. They were able to work out a *modus vivendi;* however, I have some questions how permanent this will be.

The last weeks, I noticed that the tenants were drinking a lot more than usual and felt this was related to my leaving. I tried again to reach for their negative feeling toward me without success. I asked about the drinking. One tenant did say, "Don't you know why? We love you; don't you know we all love you and will miss you?"

The main leader was never able to say this, although we had been closest, and my leaving affected her most. Finally, I asked directly if her increase in drinking was because I was leaving. She nodded, said yes, but hurriedly changed the subject and would not return to it. Another tenant said, "I'm getting drunk tonight, I'll have the shakes two days, then I'll be OK again to work on your goodbye party the last day."

Much of the foregoing was typical—the inability of tenants to express their anger, excessive drinking by alcoholics, withdrawal from the group by addicts and loners. The feverish planning of an elaborate party followed, which, in case after case, was a final tribute to the worker in that it was carried out entirely independently of him in all its elaboration. The poignant mixture of joy, intimacy, and good fellowship intermingled with the solemn ceremony of the parting gift reduced the worker and tenants alike to tears; more than one tenant expressed feeling like this: "When she cried, I was shook up. I was sure then that she cared more than I ever dreamed anyone could care about people like us."

But the morning after, she *was* really gone, and the new worker was still a shadow, often some heavy drinking and violent acting-out occurred. In one building, the distribution of police calls in response to complaints of disturbances was as follows: In each of the three weeks preceding the worker's departure—no calls; the next week—six calls; the next week—four calls; the third week—two calls. The leader of the building went on a two-week binge and only then shakily resumed her role with much less certainty.

The account in the student's material of what might be termed an "anticipatory binge" is unique. Usually tenants did not go on binges until after the worker's farewell party. This is of special importance, since "binging" as a pattern had been much reduced during the development of the program, having been replaced by chronic tippling.

The presents selected for a final gift to the workers provide a condensed portrait of the tenants' view of the worker. The symbolism embodied in these gifts accurately matched a major trait in the worker. Some of the parting gifts were a baby doll, a Jewish star, earrings belonging to the tenant leader and admired by the worker, and a notebook. What of each of these workers? The first, a very young, attractive college girl, was quite seductive with the male tenants and it was they who gave her the doll. The second worker, again a young student, was in fact preoccupied with her own group identity and learned much about this in melding with and separating from the tenants; the earrings were an expression of a deep relationship where the worker had gained much in growth and self-understanding from the dominant matriarch and vice versa. The last present was a wry comment; the worker's approach to tenants was an anxious and formal one, and she took incessant notes, probably to protect herself against the emotional impact of the experience.

No worker from the hospital was utterly ostracized, shut out of the system, although there have been a few from other agencies who were. Workers who, under a thin veneer of interest, were either deeply fearful or deeply contemptuous of tenants, were accepted by tenants. It is as though the emotional starvation for the experience offered by the workers was so intense that the particular style, technical clumsiness or inexperience, personal attributes or inhibitions of workers mattered little; as though the tenants molded the worker into an ideal image and elicited from him the behavior necessary for their needs. Gross errors of technique, rejection, or neglect by workers were forgiven or simply denied in the clamoring need to call forth whatever quantity of kindness or practical help was available. This indiscriminate and omnivorous quality characterized many tenant-worker relationships. The analogy comes to mind of the young child without a mother who wanders distraught from adult lap to lap in an endless search for mothering.

Despite the deep sense of loss, then, the new worker was quickly assimilated with the old. For a short period of time, even the names of the two workers would be interchanged. The second worker had an enormous advantage in dealing with a relatively formed group, with known personalities, and with customary activities. In two instances, the initial worker returned for a visit; the tenants, embarrassed, concealed the visit from the second worker.

Since in many instances the replacement had, by design, been the D.S.S. worker with a consolidated case load in one building, the transfer had had many special features. Tenants, as usual, were told of the plan for the D.S.S. worker to become their new project worker, and the D.S.S. worker was gradually introduced into the group settings. Usually fears were rampant that their extra and illegal activities (pilfering of petty cash, spending food money for alcohol, being addicted, having a second person living in one's room) would be discovered by the D.S.S. worker and consequently they would be "cut off" welfare. Since much deception about these issues was the rule, project workers recognized this and discussed with the tenants that some knowledge could not be shared with D.S.S. without consequences (i.e., the part-time job on the side), whereas other knowledge (alcoholism, addiction and illness) was not dangerous to share.

In one building, the tenants' reaction to the suggested transfer was that they would prefer no worker at all—a self-destructive decision, as the tenants' organization was at that point antagonistic and its indigenous leadership bitterly split. Here again after initial resistance, the changeover was far less troubled than anticipated. D.S.S. workers were readily interchangeable for hospital workers. While the power to control welfare checks created distance in some instances, it usually enhanced the helpfulness and comprehensiveness of the services rendered. For example, a request for hospital referral could, without delay, be combined with carfare allowance and restaurant allowance when necessary in the convalescent period.

Although most buildings developed their own formal leadership, thus far no building has been able to conduct its own program entirely without some intermittent help from a worker. It would appear that such buildings need some form of permanent generic social work services.

Our intervention into this system had many risks. The particular skills and personality traits of the one intervening professional became highly salient. If locating and developing rapport with indigenous leadership was unsuccessful, the worker was frozen out; if he fostered infantile dependence on himself, the social groupings were disrupted and rendered useless in carrying the therapeutic task forward. The risk of taxing fragile indigenous leaders with responsibilities beyond their capacity was ever-present.

There is also the consideration of prognosis: What is the capacity of these individuals to sustain gains, of the group to sustain cohesion? What degree of continued contact with a helping professional is necessary, if any? These questions must await further development; one may hazard the guess that some leaders will be siphoned out of the system as functioning improves, much as tenant leadership evaporates in low-income housing projects owing to upward mobility. The group's potential for replacing these leaders is unknown. A continued contact with a helping professional on an ad hoc crisis intervention basis is probably indicated, even for a stabilized population with no new input.

7

Conclusions

> There is a sense in which to set up social welfare as an end of
> actions only promotes an offensive condescension, a harsh interfer-
> ence, or an oleaginous display of complacent kindliness. . . . To
> foster conditions that widen the horizon of others and give them
> command of their own powers, so that they can find their own
> happiness in their own fashion, is the way of "social" action.
> Otherwise the prayer of a freeman would be to be left alone, and
> to be delivered, above all, from "reformers" and "kind" people.
> —JOHN DEWEY
> *Human Nature and Conduct*

Certain patterns of relationships and behavior have appeared
with consistency throughout our experience with SROs. It is
not without some qualification that we describe these patterns.
The experiences reported were not based on systematically
gathered evidence of a comparative nature. Rather, they were
impressionistic accounts by people who were themselves deeply
involved in the systems they were reporting. In all probability,
the workers distorted perceptions to protect their own role; they
may have needed to veer on the side of optimism and success
in order to guard against the depleting effects of such difficult
work. The optimism itself may have led to a self-fulfilling
prophecy, in which the workers' hope and expectation by contagion had an effect on the system. Nevertheless, there is enough
regularity to some findings to warrant confidence in their
validity.

The SRO population constitutes a subculture with a self-
assigned identity, and with mores and predictable norms unique
to it. The style of living forms a recognizable pattern in one

SRO after another in which a high degree of interconnection and mutual dependency is the rule. Despite the ugly and painful lives of these rejectees of the larger culture, a core of health has emerged; with remarkable ingenuity they have built a private culture which affords them a network of social supports. In their substitute world, some have built stable "quasi-families," have learned to protect each other and themselves from the grossest excesses of their own pathology, and have managed to survive in a situation of extreme deprivation of all forms of material goods. Gleams of altruism, love, help, wisdom, and self-knowledge have emerged from deeply embittered and damaged people. The SRO is a survival culture where chronic crises apparently stimulate highly social behavior in many of its members.

The foregoing does not imply that highly organized groups already exist. The SRO social structure can be more accurately described as a series of interlocking near-groups, with a flexible, floating membership and many partially related or unrelated marginals. Our intervention essayed a structural shift of these near-groups toward a task- and leisure-oriented formal group. The worker offered specific skills and help in enlarging the territorial group to include not only the immediate friendship cluster but the whole building. Our goal was to help the tenants adopt selectively those middle-class values which have positive and adaptive value for them—those particular values which increase their potential for survival. Other values, basic to their own style, were borrowed by the worker in a reciprocal exchange. Thus the intervention attempted an attack directly on the roots of the alienation by developing an alliance which generated hope, by gratifying urgent material and emotional needs, by increasing physical security, reducing hunger, and by creating group cohesion. For many tenants, the goal was a strengthening of ingroup ties. For a few, the goal was a detachment from the group, a lessening of the pathological bonds which prevented the individual from joining fully into the larger society. For a few others, institutionalization was usually an unsatisfactory alternative to suffering, deterioration and death.

Leadership and Extended Family Orientations

The workers who perceived themselves as helping allies of the actual power structure were able to influence a much wider social field. Those who inadvertently became competitors of the indigenous leaders tended to be helpful only to individuals marginal to all subgroups.

It is readily apparent in surveying the nine buildings that the core group most heavily committed to the programs, with minor exceptions from place to place, tended to be the Negro alcoholics, with strong, maternal figures becoming the dominant people in the recreational picture. In the different buildings this population constituted from 40 to 90 percent of the total; it is this group which has a most intensely developed mutual aid system.

In the course of program development, those who became deeply involved in the program also became close to the worker. The leaders, the active contributors, were the most accessible to change. Through identification with the worker's own views and ideals and his respectful attitude toward tenants, these more active people moved the farthest toward medical care, toward deeper and more stable relationships, and toward an orientation to the future. Participation rate and self-esteem, as judged by appearance, sociability and care of health, seemed to go hand in hand.

But an important fact emerges: The downwardly mobile middle-class people, mainly elderly Jewish, Irish and Italian single people, were uniformly resistant to the recreation aspects of our program, participated rarely and then as spectators only. With a single exception (an authoritative political activist effective as a welfare league organizer), all active leaders and organizers in every building were Negro and all but one were women. Studying the backgrounds of this group revealed that many came from the rural South and almost all had been, as children, part of extended families, shifting from parent to grandparent to other relative. The white group had small-town, primary family orientation. The difference between these two groups in attitudes toward dependence was profound. The Negroes had a well-developed capacity to help and be helped, to exchange things and feelings with generosity and joy, and to easily build an evening of singing or an impromptu talent show. Not so the whites. Several refused invitations to join Christmas dinner because they didn't need "charity," thus losing both the point of the gathering and the meal. One such lady, the house gossip, stood outside the door through many of these occasions, then accepted a plate of dinner to take to her room. Several weeks passed, then she offered to make dessert. After six months, she finally ventured to break bread and eat with the Negro tenants, who, with utmost tact, were casually but not pointedly friendly.

Thus the programs in the form we used seem tailored to the needs and strength of the Negro population. It has not yet been attempted in a predominantly white building. The capacity of whites to form socially satisfying relationships may be quite different where they are in a majority. The problems of the minority white population in Negro buildings may have another solution. Perhaps smaller homogeneous groups within a building would serve their needs better. It is likely that more staff would be necessary to do this and that there would be less of a development of mutual-aid potentials. But those who are now unreached by the program and whose needs are met on an individual casework basis might be better served.

The Managers

The SRO system demonstrates the congruence of the needs of the managers and the tenants alike, although it tends to perpetuate the pathological patterns of both. We found that the managers and tenants developed a *modus vivendi* and evolved a symbiotic relationship, both economically and interpersonally.

Understanding the managers as people, as businessmen, and as a vital functioning part of the SRO system enabled the worker to shift from a hostile reaction to him as the enemy and persecutor of tenants to a more realistic appraisal of him. To try to help the manager transform his marginal operation to a therapeutically oriented open residence became part of the worker's task.

Without the simultaneous inclusion of the managers, there appeared to be no real advancement of the program. Working with only one element of the SRO system had proven ineffective. The few examples we have had where the manager was ignored by the worker were disastrous, not only from the point of view of the manager's feelings about programs, but the tenants' feeling about the worker. In these instances the worker became an added source of conflict which fostered even greater insecurity in the tenants.

Seven out of the nine projects were deficient in work with systems other than the manager. There was a dearth of active contact with the surrounding neighbors, church groups, merchants, and block associations which could have thinned the walls of the SRO ghettos but which were not utilized.

Impact of the Program

Reliable evaluation of social change is a much desired and rarely achieved goal. While impact is extremely difficult to appraise and, because of the newness of the projects, no judgments are possible about long-term effects of the projects, some generalizations can be made about the more obvious short-term effects of these interventions. I shall therefore describe with caution our impressions of the apparent change, secured to some degree, in the nine projects. First is the problem of change in behavior and attitudes. What changes appeared in the individual tenants, the tenants participating in group experiences, and in the building as a whole?

The most obvious changes occurred in two very different kinds of individuals, the most isolated and the least isolated. A very few individuals who did not take part in the group activity at all, but who established a strong casework relationship with the worker, were dramatically helped—either to move, to get medical care, to develop friendships, or to become reconnected to family. At the other end of the spectrum were the leaders whose norms and behavior changed the most radically. The vast middle range of tenants seemed to be affected to the degree in which they participated.

Some indigenous leaders gradually developed into co-workers. They became much more highly skilled in group management, more comfortable in dealing with the larger community, and served as a source of helpful referral for the wider tenant group. As this shift took place, they began to be very busy people and they own symptomatology became much less conspicuous. The alcoholic leaders tended to drink less; two addict leaders stayed drug-free for many months. Their reference group changed as identification with the worker took place. They became upwardly mobile and several eventually moved to apartments. Three were paid as staff workers in new project buildings. Imitation of the worker's style and strategies was apparent in their work with their new tenant groups; it is also clear that many of the initial problems of the trained worker, such as exaggerated fear of contact and competition with indigenous leaders, were experienced by these former SRO leaders in their work in the new buildings.

Based upon our experience, the SRO leaders' usefulness seems to lie neither in the political arena nor in the service organizations. They are frequently too vulnerable and eccentric to tolerate job frustrations, and too debilitated physically for full-time regular employment. Also there is little incentive for most of them to give up their positions of power and authority in their SRO buildings in order to fill low-status positions in a professional world. There are exceptions, however. Of all the sixteen leaders we have worked with, two have become paid workers in other SROs and a third organized a welfare recipients' league. The majority of the leaders are valuable precisely because they live and work, albeit haphazardly, with a community of unrecognized patients who, in the usual course of events, would never be seen by any professional helper, certainly not by a psychiatrist. They perform an invaluable service, for as far as they are able, they mitigate potential disorganization in response to stress and reduce disturbed behavior and neighborhood blight. They are, in fact, the unpaid and invisible staff of nameless and unendowed halfway houses—the SROs. That such altruism can exist at all under circumstances which often produce greed, that within an intolerable living situation the creation of a "fantasy family" can occur, is a tribute to the human capacity to find and use others creatively in his struggle for survival.

The worker's problem is to seek these leaders out and increase their skills without, at the same time, separating them from the group or creating conflict or stress for them.

Caplan and Grunebaum (1) pose the question as applied to a wider range of informal care givers:

Individuals in crisis, often turn for help, not to professional care givers, but to people who live or work near them, whom they have learned to know and respect. Such informal care givers include neighbors, druggists, bartenders, hairdressers, industrial foremen, etc. They are chosen by people as confidants because of special personality gifts—capacity for empathy and understanding, an interest in their fellow men. How can we make contact with them and how can we educate them so that they give wise counsel to those in crisis who seek them out? (p. 341)

What can be said with any confidence of the impact of the programs on the buildings as a whole? The changes perceived can be described but are hard to measure. Programs tended to stabilize populations. There was much less turnover in some buildings, almost none in others. This appeared to be a result of the intervention. There was no significant change in tenants becoming economically independent. In the eight buildings where the program developed to its most elaborate form, up to three people in each became partially or fully employed as a result of the program. In viewing the population as a whole, to expect economic independence through our intervention is, at this time, out of the question. Partial economic independence might be achieved through a sheltered workshop arrangement for some tenants, but it is doubtful whether the combination of physical illness, emotional illness and life-style would ever render the great majority of these tenants able to work in the regular job market.

However, when we look at the records of police calls for the buildings, there was obviously change. In the four buildings on which we have hard data, there was a perceptible downswing of of police calls month by month as the program progressed. In two buildings the most recent tabulations show no police calls at all in the last four months. In other buildings, however, where programs served only a small ingroup, the number of police incidents did not change. It is probable that three factors enter into these statistics. As programs developed, the most antisocial, active criminals tended to need much more invisibility and therefore moved. This was true of pushers and major con men. Their moving, in turn, reduced the amount of traffic into the building and the amount of violence introduced from outside sources.

Secondly, the program tended to help reduce the violence due to internal impulsivity; that is, fighting between two tenants was more apt to be controlled by other tenants or to lessen of itself, and violent psychotic or hallucinatory episodes and suicides were, for the same reason, sometimes anticipated and these tenants cared for by others. Finally, if the program had far-reaching building-wide effects, norms of propriety were gradually adopted and enforced throughout the building. As the tenants became more acceptable to the neighborhood and their image began to improve, they themselves tended to want to control conspicuous bad behavior such as stoop loitering, bottle-throwing or screaming at night; this in turn reduced police calls and public suspicion. The norm of "good" behavior was accepted to such a degree in one building that, although the tenants openly discussed the need of the addicts to snatch purses, they formally requested them to do this at least ten blocks away, so as not to give the building a bad name.

More subtle indices of change were those that appeared to reflect increased self-esteem. The morale of many tenants seemed higher, as was evidenced by improved personal appearance and care of rooms and protectiveness of possessions. The buttons sewn on, the bed made, the frantic hunt for the irons (in scarce supply) before meetings, the wish to appear well-dressed, were increasingly characteristic of the participants in the program. Time use was changed and a future orientation began to develop, including the self-care interest, extended social relationships and greater protectiveness toward one another. Check day, customarily a time for going on binges, became a usual day. Some alcoholics shifted their drinking patterns from periodic binges to chronic tippling; this latter was also markedly reduced. In three programs, the tenants' group was able to make contact with formerly hostile block associations and other neighborhood groups and to work out a dialogue.

Rehabilitation aspects of the program involved many tenants in satisfactory social, psychiatric and medical referrals. In several buildings, nearly half the population became patients or clients successfully in new referrals. While medical referrals accounted for a large majority, psychiatric referrals also became common. No tenant accepted referral to A.A., however, and no alcoholic in any building went on the wagon. Only one addict at this writing has stayed entirely "clean" and is drug-free thirty-six months after detoxification. However, many addicts reduced their drug intake levels as a result of detoxification, and some have been repeatedly detoxified.

The Workers

Despite the wide variety of personal characteristics of workers, differing past experience, differing view of their role, professional or otherwise, there are again certain regularities which we can report with some certainty.

The workers' entrance into the buildings was, in all cases, an event of major catalytic importance for the tenants and a professional identity crisis for the workers. The entry experience was one of culture shock, in which the solution of value conflicts and the dissolution of stereotypes were the major problems. Workers dealt with these stresses primarily by denial, intellectualization or overidentification with the tenants. The entry period of acculturation, took anywhere from a few weeks to several months. The workers varied greatly in the degree to which they could attain a congruence of expectations with those of the tenants or were able to adjust sufficiently to remain in the system. But some were much more successful than others in creating a strong bond between themselves and the tenants. It is my impression that the higher the social class of the workers, the less conflicts there were in the opening phase. This apparent correlation needs future systematic study.

Ultimately, it was the workers' capacity to find the positive potential for growth in the tenants that enabled the tenants to develop faith in the worker. After this, hope in themselves emerged and evolved, by small degrees, into change. The workers needed to preserve a vision, an image of the tenants, as they might become or of the building as it might become. They also needed to envision a strengthened, expanded and enhanced mutual aid system. Then, through identification, the tenants sought out this vision for themselves and were able to modify their behavior and feel somewhat less apathetic, hopeless, unprotected and at the mercy of fate. The formation of the group was a by-product of this essential first bond of trust and was essential to its early beginnings. As the group had success in mastering small pieces of experience—attaining a recreation room, having a dinner, confronting the manager, taking a trip—the group itself began to provide its own source of love and security to a greater degree, and the relationship to the worker, while never fully dispensable, became much less important.

While some workers saw the more self-directing autonomous side of the SRO tenants, others initially saw the infantile and pathological side. Most ultimately arrived at a balanced perception. If they stressed the pathology, protective and custodial solutions predominated. Those who stressed the more adult qualities in tenants tended to stress social change solutions. The more balanced the view, the greater the impact, as the SRO tenants are surely no single entity but a range of individuals, some of whom are in desperate need of custodial care, while others seek expression of their most mature selves.

As identification with the SRO culture developed, workers sometimes also lost sight of the justified anger of the surrounding community. It was difficult for some workers to bear in mind that there is a balance of rights to be considered here—the right of the internal culture to live within the norms it sets for itself, and the importance of not interfering with the rights and norms of the larger culture outside.

By training, agency identification and personal preference, each social worker tends to favor one of the three social work methods: casework, group work or community organization. The dominant orientation of the project workers or the agencies involved in SRO work tends to shape the way the worker relates to the tenants and the goals they develop, which then may become self-fulfilling prophecies. Most SRO workers have had a group-work orientation, a few were caseworkers and one was a community organizer.

The consequences were striking. The caseworker tended to treat each tenant separately and privately, building between himself and the client a unique, confidential relationship. Each tenant shared the worker with no one. It resulted in some solutions to serious problems such as medical care, job training or moving. Only secondarily was the tenant's social relationship in the building affected, weakened or strengthened. Since SRO dwellers seem so pathological, it was in many caseworkers' judgments a place to leave, unaware that essential social bonds, however rudimentary or bizarre, existed. In talking to caseworkers, tenants often stressed the negative aspect of living in their buildings. The worker then made elaborate and time-consuming plans to help the tenant move, only to find that the tenant inexplicably had "changed his mind" or didn't "feel well enough just now."

The community organization approaches to SROs attempted to organize the tenants to insist on more adequate living facilities, better care from welfare, better hospital treatment. The SRO population is easily led. To please any worker, a core group of tenants will march and protest. But their effort is unsustained, their view of their trouble parochial. One community organizer encouraged a group to demonstrate before City Hall before they had formed a solid ingroup. It was a minor disaster. Some got lost; others began to drink while there; two, physically too weak, collapsed, and the rest struggled home exhausted and confused.

Political awareness and action for SRO dwellers is the culmination, not a point of beginning. Before issues can be generalized and fought for there must be anger, and before anger can emerge, hope must be generated, and a sense of justice, based on self-worth. So SRO programs must begin at the beginning, or in the social work dictum, "begin where the client is"— the SRO tenant is not yet a revolutionary; he is too sick, too malnourished and in too much personal pain. These problems have priority. Political action becomes a positive force at a later time in their development as a group.

The group workers tended to make the process of group interaction the point from which other activities radiated, and therefore to place priority on finding or forming groups. Simultaneously, individual emergencies of tenants occurred within the group and out of it—and had to be handled. The group worker then tried to take both roles. But the second, or casework, role changed. Because of his knowledge of the social network, he could make use of the mutual aid system to help the individual. Though it was not achieved in all buildings, constant efforts were made to include sympathetic tenants in solving the individual's problem and to ask them to take on some of the helping responsibility. The worker thus formalized the giving-helping impulse and dignified it to include actions requiring increasingly greater skill—accompanying a sick tenant to the hospital and helping with admission, arranging by telephone for ambulances, speaking to relatives, arranging for burial of a tenant, appearing in court—all frightening and unfamiliar, but possible with the worker's support. A series of case aides thus emerged who could handle crises and negotiate for services from outside systems. In the setting where the group worker was alone in the building, he was forced to do this, or become so buried in individual crises that the group development suffered. Then, too, the personality of the worker alone in one building tended to create a large family constellation in which all shared one worker in common.

Thus group workers had to expand their role to include the skills of all three areas of specialization. The more skill they could bring to bear to integrate the three methods, the more effective they were as SRO workers.

8

Recommendations

The [housing] projects are important not only for themselves; they are also important for their impact on the rest of the city. And perhaps their most important effect has been in upsetting the balance of the slums. Large numbers of normal families living in slums (the chief candidates for the projects) have been withdrawn from them, leaving the remaining slums to become the homes of the old, the criminal, the mentally unbalanced, the most depressed and miserable and deprived. The slums now contain the very large families that are not eligible for public housing because they would overcrowd it; the families that have been ejected from the projects (or were never admitted) for being antisocial; those who have either recently arrived in the city and hardly adapted to urban life, or those who may have been here a long time but never adapted; as well as the dope peddlers and users, the sex perverts and criminals, the pimps and prostitutes whom the managers reject or eject to protect the project population. . . . And what after all are we to do with the large numbers of people emerging in modern society who are irresponsible and depraved? The worthy poor create no serious problem—nothing that money cannot solve. But the unworthy poor? No one has come up with the answers.

—NATHAN GLAZER and DANIEL P. MOYNIHAN
Beyond the Melting Pot

The Housing Maintenance Code of New York City, passed in July, 1967 (Sect. D 26–33.11), is designed to shut down all SROs in New York City in which more than six persons share a bathroom by July 14, 1977. Its drafters reasoned that there would be no need for SRO housing by that time, assuming that the population they house would not then be in existence.

On the contrary, there are several reasons why the SRO population might well expand with time. Migration into New York City will continue from the rural areas in the future, with an influx of persons of minimal vocational skills and education. Rising unemployment of the marginal labor force due to automation is likely to add numbers of these workers to the population. There is an absolute number of permanently marginal single people in urban centers: the crippled, blind, alcoholic, mentally retarded, and mentally ill. State hospitals, medical institutions for the chronically ill, and prisons are all moving in the direction of early return to the community and aftercare services there. The elderly alone will live longer. State hospital dischargees will be maintained on tranquilizers in the community. As hospital expenses increase and medical advances are made, patients will increasingly have shorter hospital stays. Part of the aftercare convalescent and parole population will filter down into SRO housing, swelling the existing pool of SRO dwellers. In the long range, the SRO population will inevitably increase.

The enforcement of the code which disenfranchises SRO housing without equivalent housing construction in a situation of a growing, not shrinking, population, could produce a homeless beggar culture more reminiscent of Dickens' London than twentieth-century America. Just as the 1960s' regulation of the New York City Buildings Department for the closing of 20 percent of SROs each year was quietly dropped as the consequences became visible, so this code may be rendered unenforceable as its impact becomes apparent. As reported in the New York *Times* (19) already one tenant organization has begun court tests of eviction notices tendered by their landlord as his response to notices of Code violation and notification that he would be subject to court prosecution for continuing to use his building as an SRO dwelling, in violation of that provision requiring that he should have filed plans for renovation of his building to provide the sufficient proportion of bathrooms by Jan. 1, 1968. Widespread protests have elicited sympathetic recognition by the Lindsay administration of the need to assist landlords with low-interest municipal or state loans to enable them to upgrade their buildings so as to continue to serve this population.

The New York City Planning Board has had the foresight and financial resources to pay for a study of the SRO situation. This report (2) may influence the combined Departments of Housing, Welfare, Hospitals and Health to create a coordinated plan for this population that is certain to be a permanent part of the metropolitan scene.

While one kind of effort at amelioration of the SRO problem has been described here, there are many others to be explored. In fact, new knowledge about the buildings as marginally functioning systems raises many questions. What further responsibility does a city have for the housing, social and health needs of this population? What might be an ideal housing pattern? What discharge and aftercare plans of hospitals and prisons would adequately break into the cycle of reinstitutionalization of homeless patients and prisoners? What legislative changes are indicated in revision of the regulations regarding SRO licensing, management and maintenance? What in-building services for sick and disabled welfare recipients must be provided beyond maintenance on a sustenance dole? The community at large as well as the professional community have responsibilities for effecting change in these areas.

Our recommendations stem from our conviction that a way of life has evolved in SROs with both destructive and constructive aspects. The destructive, blighting ones can be altered and the constructive ones strengthened when a quality of helping relationships and a range of effective services are brought into the buildings. As housing units they can be absorbed into the middle-class surround, under specific circumstances to be described.

Between 60 and 70 percent of the SROs are in fair to good physical condition and usually have few social problems because the tenants are employed blue-collar workers or students. We offer no specific recommendations for these buildings and their population. For the scattered few (3 to 5 percent) which are dilapidated beyond repair, there is no alternative but to raze them. The remaining buildings are those which concern us here. These comprise about 25 percent of the total (approximately 125 buildings in New York City, each containing about 120 tenants). They are in poor but not dilapidated condition and chiefly house welfare recipients (about 15,000 tenants).

Any amelioration of the barely functioning SROs must take into account the three intertwined factors: the deteriorated physical structure, the social system of the tenants, and the social and economic reality of management. Changes in any one of these affects the other two.

The Buildings

What is ideal housing for this group of people? What kind of physical plant provides optimal living space for their physical and social needs? It is our strong impression that in size and physical layout, the SROs have many advantages. A typical old-law six-floor tenement with a tenant population of 100 to 150 is large enough for a heterogeneous population to find common ground, yet small enough so that most faces, if not names, are familiar to all. In one much larger building of over 400 tenants, no one knew with certainty who lived there and who did not, and social contacts between tenants were minimal. The central elevator and lobby with the open location of the manager's office increase the visibility of tenants to one another and to management. These six- to eight-room wings are small enough to be conducive to social interaction and the common kitchens increase this potential, while preserving the option of privacy of the tenants' own rooms. The physical layout also permits the maintenance staff to have daily access to the rooms; they therefore can become a source of help when needed. By contrast, if each person had a one-room apartment with an inside kitchen, tenants who became ill or psychotic could remain lost to view for a very long time.

The common bathroom is another matter. A great many tenants resent sharing so intimate a facility, and private sinks and toilets would ease this indignity and strain.

However, we suggest that every wing of every floor have a small common living room. In addition in such buildings, part of the first floor should be set aside for a large recreation room, offices for incoming services such as welfare workers, visiting nurses' service and medical care, and a small two- or three-bed infirmary for temporarily ill tenants who need nursing care but not hospitalization. In the basement, a kitchen should be created to prepare and serve one main meal daily. This meal would again be optional but prepaid. The kitchen staff could be part-time employees drawn from the tenant population itself. In a similar plan for optimal SRO housing, Levy (9) suggests a 20-story building with 500 residential rooms, a large social hall with a steam table to serve one meal a day prepared elsewhere and delivered to the building, to be served to the tenants, and an in-building social rehabilitation program.

These suggested innovations are structurally feasible in the typical six-story SRO building and involve conversion of some existing rental room units into community space.

The Tenants

Who should live in these well-maintained SROs? Should there be a mix of pathologies, a mix of classes, a mix of ethnic groups and of ages, or should alcoholics, addicts, the physically ill and handicapped live in homogeneous groups? Should there be mixed housing for both those who need more protection and care and for those who need little, or should those who need more services live in separate groups?

The heterogeneous population spread in the existing SROs has many positive aspects. The mixture of ages, classes and races provides a lively matrix, despite the fact that many of the patho-logical and ethnic groups tend to withdraw socially from others. Contact with other tenants is a potential area of stimulation and interest. Witness the depressing social atmosphere of old-age homes, convalescent homes and public housing projects in which planned homogeneity results in environmental boredom. From time to time, some observers have asserted that the clustering of so many people with pathology reinforces their illness, and have made the suggestion that marginal, unattached single people be layered and scattered in among family dwellings. We disagree. This would rob these marginal members of the community of the last hope that they have of creating a social system of their own, and would leave them isolates among people who would shun them socially and would share with them no common interests.

The housing needs of the SRO population fall into several categories. There are a few tenants who, if public housing restrictions were relaxed, might find living in an apartment in public housing congenial. These are upwardly mobile persons with a basically middle-class orientation. There are also a few people who are barely surviving in SROs in avoidance of institutional care. It is a moot point whether their survival or happiness would be increased by placement in a state hospital, an old-age home or a chronic disease hospital. For many of them, the idea of institutionalization has become synonymous with death, as it often, in reality is. These tenants require more services than the SRO at best can provide, but they do not need formal institutionalization. Custodial and protective homes should be operated under public auspices for this portion of the population. Based on our experience, about 5 percent of the SRO tenants require such care. Their problems occur in such combinations (e.g., a blind, retarded, nonpsychotic alcoholic) as to make them ineligible for custodial institutions, but they cannot function adequately in the unstaffed SRO.

For this purpose, the Department of Social Services should buy or lease two or more SROs of 100 to 150 units, each to be operated on a demonstration basis under its auspices, with special services provided for the tenants. Tenants should be selected from those leaving institutions, or already residing in SROs, who require the equivalent of long-term homemaker service or close supervision, but who do not require complete nursing care or intensive social control in a closed setting. Residence should be voluntary in these SRO halfway houses. The D.S.S. should provide on-site meals, homemakers' services, professional and social services, and arrange for and coordinate visiting medical and nursing services.

The vast majority of tenants could remain in SROs providing a series of changes are made in addition to the structural ones indicated above. These SROs could continue under private ownership with economic incentives to the owners not only to maintain minimum standards but to go beyond them. The following recommendations are made:

1. The 1977 SRO termination law should be altered; it should stimulate rational redistribution of the SRO population into sound SRO facilities with integrated service programs throughout the City. Section D26–33.07 (1968) of the N.Y.C. Administrative Code permits the building or rehabilitation of SRO's if they are *either* owned and operated without profit by an educational, religious or charitable institution as a residence for the aged, or for working girls or women, or for working boys or men; *or* "owned, operated or used by The City of New York."

2. Housing codes for these SROs should be expanded to include such items as furnishings, mattresses and linens, working order of stoves, refrigerators, lamps, etc. There should be strict provisions concerning the providing of security, garbage disposal, cleaning, hall and lobbly lighting and general repair. Twenty-four-hour supervision of the door and lobby of the building should be required by the owner, lessee or manager.

3. Rent increases on a sliding scale proportionate to the increased services rendered should be authorized by the N.Y.C. Department of Rent and Housing Maintenance to those landlords who maintain buildings at higher than nominal levels in security, maintenance, furnishings, provision of recreation space and cooperation with in-building service programs. This would not only offset the higher maintenance costs but should provide a net income gain to cooperating landlords.

4. Low-interest municipal or state loans should be made available to owners who wish to rehabilitate SRO buildings by installing private bathrooms, lounges on each floor in each wing, basement kitchens, a large recreation hall, im-

proved lighting and ventilation, and modernized heating plants, plumbing and electricity.

5. Inspections should be required every three months by teams from the municipal departments which share sectors of responsibility in enforcing the municipal codes governing SRO buildings, including the Departments of Social Services, Sanitation, Fire Prevention, and Housing Maintenance. Any municipal department whose standards are not being met should be authorized to penalize the landlord through the withholding of rental income until the conditions are corrected in any building with a record of poor upkeep. The Department of Social Services should have the legal authority to withhold the payment of rent to the landlord in the same way.

Program of Social Services

One lead agency should have the authority to structure the programs of social and rehabilitative services in these buildings. The Department of Social Services seems the obvious choice for mounting a major city-wide program to include all SRO buildings where over 40 percent of the tenants are welfare recipients and to have that building as a whole considered a therapeutic target for the Department. All other services should become ancillary to the chief agency. Visiting nursing services, medical visits and homemaker services should be provided to each building on a regular, not emergency, basis and should be included in the financial planning for the work of the lead agency as part of the basic therapeutic team.

Two D.S.S. social workers should staff each building of 100 tenants. One should be a specialist in individual casework; the second, who should assume overall direction for the work of the therapeutic team, should be a generically trained social worker who works with groups in the building, the tenants' association and other community agencies. The target should be the total building, including non-welfare tenants, management and staff, and the surrounding neighborhood.

The Department of Social Services should provide the money
necessary for running a recreation-rehabilitation program at a
minimum of $1.00 per tenant per month. Accountability for the
expenditure of this money should rest solely with the tenants'
association. The daily food program and any experimental
projects such as building-based sheltered workshops should be
financed also by the D.S.S.

Present D.S.S. workers need intensive professional training
and supervision in order to become generic workers able to
assume responsibility for heading the basic therapeutic team.
In our experience, the idealized SRO worker has functioned
generically. He has had to shift quickly from the individual to
the group to systems and community work. In a single day he
may instruct a tenant as to how to make a telephone call or
facilitate his requests for service, discuss with the manager his
troubles with an overloaded electrical system, sit with tenant
leaders while they discuss the afternoon's building-wide meeting
(suggesting ways of involving silent tenants and controlling
others), participate in the meeting where he helps clarify issues,
then go with the tenants' association president to a church group
meeting around the corner to talk about the building and its program, inviting the group to participate in it.

An idealized summary of the development of an SRO social
service project under D.S.S. direction can be described as
follows:

Typical Sequence for Intervention in a
Single Room Occupancy Building

I. Opening Phase
   1. Securing information about the history, structural status
      and reputation of the building.
   2. Beginning contact includes manager, maids, super.
   3. Negotiating with manager.
   4. Socializing on stoop, in lobby.
   5. Asking one tenant to lead worker to others.
   6. Knocking on doors.
   7. Giving service in medical, psychiatric and/or personal
      emergency.

      8. Beginning location of social subclusters.

II. Contract Phase

      1. Participating in group life, making explicit self-help capacity.

      2. Setting up team relationships with leaders, planning with them.

      3. Defining of common task and reciprocal roles.

      4. Holding initial group meeting: small group, leader group or building-wide group.

      5. Negotiating about recreation room with manager.

III. Work Phase

      1. Planning and holding building-wide meetings.

      2. Locating areas of common interest and work.

      3. Working together to active goals of mutual pleasure or problem solving.

        a. First activity tends to have attributes of low anxiety and high gratification, i.e., recreation, food, TV.

        b. Subsequent content tends to become more problem- and process-oriented, i.e., use of money, referrals, D.S.S. and managerial relations, and control of disruption and violence.

      Phase problems: 1. Subgroup territoriality in tenants' organization.

                    2. Worker-leader competition.

                    3. Transfer of leader's power and interest beyond building as lieutenants are developed.

                    4. Gradual shift of responsibility for organization and money, etc., to variety of leaders.

IV. Transfer: Separation of Worker and Tenants

      1. Preparation by worker.

      2. Working through mourning while worker is still there.

      3. Shift of responsibility to new worker.

Epilogue

The SRO dwellers are known to us because they have become visible; through historical chance their homes are islands of poverty in the midst of middle-class neighborhoods. If these same slum hotels were in the Bowery, the SRO dwellers would in all probability have remained in limbo and we might never have come to participate in their lives.

I have tried to describe the tapestry of their lives as we perceived it: the brutality and suffering inextricably mingled with love, laughter and a will to survive as thinking and feeling human beings. In spite of the pain and ugliness, these single, sick and deviant people affirm their humanity in their expressions of generosity, humor, pity, and connectedness to each other. This book has attempted to convey a measure of the depth and meaning of their limbo—the pointless stoicism of their physical and emotional pain, and its counterpart in the creative use of their isolation to produce a community. They are a monument to man's capacity to endure as a social being, even when he is deprived of the supports considered vital—the dignity of economic worth, the security of possessions, the pride of skill, the comfort and anchor of family, the beauty of objects and of nature. Yet he has made a home, and if he is lucky, he has a make-believe mother, buddy, protector, sister, brother, child— he has a family.

To help SRO tenants, we must perceive and preserve their achievement, and use our own loving qualities as caretakers to expand it, so that our altruism, respect and concern matches and enhances theirs. If we enter his home environment sensitively, looking to enhance the mutual aid system already in operation there, his social setting can become a potentially powerful lever in his becoming a person with self-respect and dignity.

The History of SROs in New York City

A large park divides Manhattan into two major residential areas. The East Side is well-heeled, Republican and middle- to upper-class, with a few islands of ethnic ghettos. The West Side, encompassing 250 square blocks from 59th Street to 125th Street, needs new soles, is Democratic and lower- to upper-middle-class. It is home to a sprawling mixture of economic classes and racial groups; the poor and the wealthy, black, white, Oriental and Spanish-speaking live cheek by jowl. It is here that SROs are concentrated and where, for historical reasons, they have achieved their notoriety. The West Side has six north-south avenues; three are largely commercial, and three were, at the turn of the century, highly fashionable residential avenues with high-rise apartment buildings. These avenues were peopled in turn by affluent Anglo-Saxon Protestants, Irish Catholics and Jews. The cross streets have contiguous brownstones and a few six-story tenements which housed their poorer neighbors. As the flight to the suburbs gained momentum in the thirties, the West Side as a whole gradually declined, keeping however its characteristic separation of classes. The three residential avenues are still upper-middle-class, while many of the side streets have become Negro and Puerto Rican ghettos for blue-collar families. Two commercial avenues have become largely Puerto Rican, with the shadows of their Irish and Jewish history reflected in little-used churches and synagogues, Irish bars and Kosher meat markets. Residual residents of these two groups drifted into what became SROs—aging and sick

147

white people, downwardly mobile stragglers left behind as their families moved out and away.

In the New York City Multiple Dwelling Law of 1929 (Subdivision 6, Section 4) an SRO was defined as "the occupancy by one or two persons of a single room, or of two or more which are joined together, separated from all other rooms within an apartment in a multiple dwelling, so that the occupant or occupants thereof reside separately and independently of the other occupant or occupants of the same apartment. . . ." A rooming house is a one- or two-family dwelling (brownstone, for example) converted to furnished room use, as a temporary place of stay. It is a room in a house of another, used as a place of residence, where sleeping accommodations are provided. The definition of a residential hotel is a little more complex. A residential hotel is a multiple dwelling that provides lodging and usually meals, entertainment and various personal services for the public. The units are self-contained—that is, have kitchen and bathroom facilities (12).

The real beginning of the SRO phenomenon, the conspicuous clustering of deviant single people in specific buildings, began in World War II in the early forties. The war produced a major housing shortage in New York City due to an influx of workers manning war plants and servicemen. These workers strained normal hotel facilities beyond their capacity. It became profitable to convert certain types of buildings to rooming accommodations. On the side streets, usually mid-block, were six-story structures, old-law and new-law tenements which were built at the turn of the century. The typical shape is that of an "H," the core containing an elevator shaft and stairs, with the four arms each containing six to eight rooms, or four apartments to each floor. These were easily converted; that is, the rooms of an apartment were rented as a series of single-room units to six to eight tenants, sharing what was to become the community kitchen and bath. The conversion costs were little in some cases, entailing only keeping the apartment door permanently open or adding a corridor wall. These buildings came to be known as SROs.

This space was occupied rapidly by servicemen and factory workers, many migrating from the South and Puerto Rico. The postwar economic boom stimulated continued major population movement into the city from rural areas. The SRO soon became a haven for very poor families trying to get a start in the city. A man or, more

TYPICAL S.R.O. FLOOR PLAN

| Bedroom | Bedroom | Kitchen | Bedroom | Bedroom | Kitchen | Bedroom |

| Bedroom | Bath | Bedroom | | Bedroom | Bath | Bedroom |

Bedroom

Elevator

Bedroom

Bedroom

Bedroom

Bedroom

Bedroom

| Bedroom | Bath | Bedroom | W.C. | Bedroom | Bath | Bedroom |

| Bedroom | Kitchen | Bedroom | Bedroom | Bedroom | Kitchen |

often, a woman would arrive, get a job as a domestic, restaurant or garment worker, and then send for his or her family. The least successful were caught in the SROs; here whole families lived in one room and slept in shifts. Those who failed to become economically independent due to lack of skill, education or health became welfare recipients. By the middle fifties, an unplanned and unwilling interdependence between the Department of Welfare and the more marginal SROs emerged. Both families and single people were referred to SROs by welfare centers for "temporary" housing, which tended to become permanent. Former prisoners, mental hospital dischargees, and homeless convalescents from other hospitals landed, usually without notice and in great numbers, at the welfare centers with nowhere else to go. Housed in SROs with no sustaining rehabilitative services, they became caught in a cycle of readmission, usually in the midst of a crisis. Public concern about families living in dilapidated SROs found expression in a 1960 law (Multiple Dwelling Law No. 6–D26–321, 1960), forbidding rental of rooms to all tenants with children by 1965. The Neighborhood Conservation Bureau (N.C.B.) and the Department of Welfare (in New York City, the Department of Social Services, D.S.S.) together took on the burden of gradually rehousing these families. They were replaced by more single people; the concentration of the unattached individuals in the SRO became ever more marked.

The SRO-type population probably lived on New York's Skid Row, the Bowery before the conversion of the buildings during World War II. The Bowery was a far more heterogeneous and populous place at the beginning of this century than it is today. Its population has dwindled from estimates varying between 26,000 and 65,000 in 1915 (17) to fewer than 6,000 in 1964 (11). Once it was a pool of seasonal and transient manpower, a home for soldiers, sailors, migrant workers, people temporarily down on their luck, displaced victims of disasters, and the people who today occupy SROs. Specialized services such as sailor homes, veterans' hospitals, and improved welfare allowances funneled funds and housing to many of these groups; only the residual hard-core alcoholics now remain, most of whom are over fifty. It is the chronically disabled residual of this population which has moved uptown into SROs, partly because of the fortuitous conversion of buildings into SROs. As wartime housing pressures eased, the SRO space became available to them. Meanwhile the maximum monthly wel-

fare rent allowance for the single person rose from *$45* in *1940* to
$90 in *1968*.

Because of the rapid deterioration of the West Side, particularly
on the side streets, it became a target for planning efforts by the
Housing and Redevelopment Board, beginning in 1960. Housing
conditions were evaluated and discrete geographic areas were desig-
nated to be handled in three separate ways: 1) Renewal areas, in
which a major part of the housing was dilapidated and renovation
was economically unfeasible. Selective razing of whole blocks, including many SROs, has been carried out between 1960 and the
present. 2) Service areas, which were sufficiently deteriorated that
a holding operation of five to ten years' duration was planned, with
complete renewal as an ultimate goal. 3) Conservation areas, where
little demolition was necessary but renovation and increased local
participation in upgrading the neighborhood was planned. The
latter two types of areas, which contain most of the remaining SROs,
are under the auspices of Neighborhood Conservation Bureau, a
subdivision of the Housing and Redevelopment Board charged with
the improvement of the physical and social environments of deteriorating neighborhoods.

It was this agency which was the first to recognize the SRO as a
local and city-wide physical and social problem. By the time N.C.B.'s
local offices began to operate, the more pernicious SROs had begun
to produce neighborhood blight, repelling middle-class families and
depressing real estate values. This, in turn, had led to urban renewal
projects which by their nature displaced the SRO population. A
heartbreaking and expensive pattern emerged, where each area tried
to displace its most undesirable population, only to have blight
spread into adjacent areas.

In 1968 in New York City there were 594 buildings legally classified as SROs, providing 3,179 apartments and 32,669 single units
(13). On the basis of these figures, the number of people then
living in SROs can be estimated at over 40,000. Four hundred and
eighteen such buildings were in Manhattan, most of them on the
West Side, 110 in the Bronx, 63 in Brooklyn, 3 in Queens, and
none in Richmond. This represents a decrease of SRO units from
the preceding five years, due to four factors: 1) Urban Renewal
razed and converted all SROs in its areas; 2) to the north, in the
Morningside Heights area, expansion by educational institutions
necessitated rapid acquisition of land and buildings—at least 19 of

31 SROs in that area were razed or reconverted as a result (10);
3) anger and political action by neighborhood groups caused un-
favorable publicity and pressure on managers to sell, reconvert, or
upgrade specific buildings in the remaining areas: 4) pressures by
Neighborhood Conservation Bureau forced landlords into either
correcting building code violations or bankruptcy, sale, or conversion.

The great majority of SROs are not dilapidated and are respon-
sibly managed. The "better" SROs usually have a selective screen-
ing policy which excludes tenants with severe social problems. These
buildings tend to house blue-collar single people or couples, elderly
white single people of respectable background, self-supporting or on
welfare, and students in those SROs near the universities.

But some are in such poor condition as to constantly mitigate
against social rehabilitation and severely limit and negate the effect
of health and welfare services. These buildings house those least able
to care for themselves. In this book I have set aside the legal definition of an SRO as a licensed building meeting certain requirements.
The term SRO has referred to those 50 or more buildings in which
marginality of the physical structure, the management, and the
single, unattached tenant population coalesce to form a self-rein-
forcing structure of internal pathology and external blight.

Bibliography

1. Caplan, G., and Grunebaum, H., "Perspectives on Primary Prevention," *Archives of General Psychiatry,* Vol. 17, Sept. 1967.
2. Center for New York City Affairs, New School for Social Research, N.Y.C., *Report for Community Planning Board #7: Single Room Occupancy Problems on Manhattan's West Side* (mimeo), Dec. 1968.
3. Feldstiner, J. P., *Detached Work.* Toronto, Canada: University of Toronto Press, Feb. 1965.
4. Glazer, Nathan, and Moynihan, Daniel Patrick, *Beyond the Melting Pot: The Negroes, Puerto Ricans, Jews, Italians, & Irish of New York City.* Cambridge, Mass.: The M.I.T. Press, 1963.
5. Gorky, Maxim, *Years of My Childhood.* Baltimore, Md.: Penguin Books, 1966.
6. Jellinek, E. M., "Cultural Differences in the Meaning of Alcoholism," *Society, Culture and Drinking Patterns,* D. Pittman and C. Snyder, eds., Chapter 22, pp. 362–388. New York: John Wiley and Sons, 1962.
7. Jones, Maxwell, *The Therapeutic Community.* New York: Basic Books, 1953.
8. Lefkowitz, Nathan, *A Case Study of an Extended Family Among Ward-Outcast Slum Dwellers* (in manuscript), New York, Sept. 1968.
9. Levy, Herbert, "Optimum S.R.O. Housing: An Unrecognized Urban Housing Need," *Journal of Housing,* Vol. 25, No. 11, Dec. 1968.
10. Morningside Heights, Inc., New York, "S.R.O. Study" (mimeo), 1967.
11. Nash, Patricia, and Nash, George, "A Preliminary Estimate of the Population and Housing of the Bowery in New York City." New York, Bureau of Applied Social Research (mimeo), Columbia University, 1964.
12. New York City Department of Buildings, *Building Maintenance Code,* 1965.

13. New York City Department of Buildings, *Statistical Report* Sept. 1965.

14. New York City Department of Social Services, Bureau of Statistics, New York, 1965 (mimeo).

15. New York City Department of Social Services, "Amsterdam-St. Luke's Hospital S.R.O. Projects," Unit 22, Amsterdam Welfare Center, June 1968 (mimeo).

16. New York City Housing and Redevelopment Board, "World of 207" (mimeo), Feb. 1966.

17. New York City Municipal Lodging House, *The Men We Lodge*, New York: Municipal Lodging House, 1915.

18. New York City Youth Board, New York City, *Reaching the Fighting Gang*, 1960.

19. New York *Times*, "City Acts to Ease Roomer's Plight," Dec. 8, 1968.

20. Orwell, George, *Down and Out in Paris and London* (1933). New York: Berkley Publishing Corp., 1959.

21. Rapoport, Robert, *Community as Doctor*. London: Tavistock Publications, 1959.

22. Rose, Arnold, "Interest in the Living Arrangements of the Urban Unattached," *American Journal of Sociology*, Vol. 53, 1947–48.

23. Scheidlinger, S., "Social Group Work and Group Psychotherapy," *Social Work*, Vol. 1, No. 3, July 1956.

24. Schwartz, William, "The Social Worker in the Group," *New Perspectives on Services to Groups: Theory, Organization and and Practice*. New York: N.A.S.W., 1961, pp. 7–34.

25. Shapiro, Joan, "Dominant Leaders Among Slum Hotel Residents," *American Journal of Ortho-psychiatry*, Spring, 1969.

26. Siris, Sam, "The Underutilization of Medical Facilities by the Residents of an SRO Dwelling" (mimeo). New York: St. Luke's Hospital, Aug. 1967.

27. Sole, Harold, "Annual Report of Site Management Division for 1961," New York City Housing Authority, 1962 (mimeo).

28. Stokes, Janet, "Friendship Patterns of the 'Urban Unattached,'" manuscript submitted for publication, Dec. 1968.

29. Stokes, Janet, working paper on the Dimensions of Participation in a Slum Hotel Recreation-Rehabilitation Program (mimeo). New York: St. Luke's Hospital, 1967.

30. Stone, Gregory, "Drinking Styles and Social Arrangements," *Society, Culture and Drinking Patterns*, D. Pittman and C. Snyder, eds., Chapter 7, pp. 121–140. New York: John Wiley and Sons, 1962.

31. Wallace, Samuel, *Skid Row as a Way of Life,* Totowa, N.J.: Bedminster Press, 1965.
32. Yablonsky, L., *The Violent Gang,* New York: Macmillan Co., 1962.
33. Zerwick, Lillian, "The Public Agency as a Team Participant in Providing Mental Health Services," Amsterdam Services Center of the New York City Department of Social Services, American Orthopsych. Conference, March 1968 (mimeo).
34. Zorbaugh, Harvey, "Dweller in Furnished Rooms: An Urban Type," *The Urban Community,* Ernest Burgess, ed. Chicago University Press, 1929.